# Train Hard, Win Easy
## The Kenyan Way

*Toby Tanser*

Foreword by John Manners

TAFNEWS PRESS
Book Division of Track & Field News, Inc.

First published in 1997 by Tafnews Press,
Book Division of Track & Field News,
2570 El Camino Real, Suite 606
Mountain View, CA 94040 USA.

Second printing, February 1998, updates all statistics,
p. 17-30, and the first page statistics of each event chapter
in Part II, but no other adjustments (to take into account
the1997 outdoor season) were made in the text.

Standard book number: 0-911521-50-X

Printed in the United States of America

Cover design and production: Teresa Tam

Cover—the 1995 World Cross Country
Championships, Durham, England.
Photo by John Burles.

# Contents

Foreword by John Manners ............................................................ 5
Introduction ............................................................................. 11
Maps ......................................................................................... 12

## Part I—Running in Kenya

A Brilliant Record of Success ...................................................... 17
    Kenyan Medalists in Major Championships .......................... 17
    IAAF World Cross Country Championships .......................... 25
    Track & Field News #1 Rankings 1966-1996 ....................... 27
    Kenyan World Record Setters ............................................. 27
    Boston Marathon Winners ................................................. 28
    Top Ten Rankings 1987-1996 ............................................ 29
    1996 Track & Field News World Rankings .......................... 30
Training Scenes ......................................................................... 31
    Training in the Schools ..................................................... 33
    The Ups and Downs of Hard Training ................................ 36
The Varieties of Training ............................................................ 38
    In-Season Training ............................................................ 38
    Interval Training ............................................................... 39
    Tempo Training ................................................................. 41
    The Long Run .................................................................. 42
    Hill Work ......................................................................... 43
    Rest and Recovery ........................................................... 44
    Rest During the Hard Training Period ............................... 47
    Strength Training .............................................................. 48
    Personal Themes .............................................................. 49
Economics of Training ................................................................ 51
The Training Camp ..................................................................... 53
    The Armed Forces Training Camp ..................................... 55
    The Iten Training Camp .................................................... 58
    The National Training Camp for the World Cross
        Country Championships ................................................ 60
    The Barcelona Steeplechase Training Camp ...................... 64
The Kenyan Diet ........................................................................ 66
    Key Diet Ingredients of a Typical Rift Valley Resident ......... 67
    Pills and Supplements ....................................................... 68
    Typical Daily Diets ............................................................ 69
    Diet on the Road .............................................................. 71

A Blood Link! ............................................................................................................... 72
Kenyan Running Success—Some Roots and Reasons ........................................ 74
    Tribal Affiliations ................................................................................................ 74
    Altitude ................................................................................................................. 77
    The Weather ........................................................................................................ 77
    A Walking Heritage ............................................................................................ 78
    Tradition and Belief ............................................................................................ 79
    Attitude Not Altitude ......................................................................................... 80
Born to Run? .............................................................................................................. 81
A Day at the Races .................................................................................................... 84

# Part II—Profiles of Champions

Kenyan Pioneers ....................................................................................................... 95
    Kip Keino ............................................................................................................. 95
    Henry Rono ......................................................................................................... 99
    Ibrahim Hussein ............................................................................................... 101
    Mike Musyoki .................................................................................................... 102
    Other Pioneers .................................................................................................. 104
The Coaches .............................................................................................................. 107
    Brother Colm O'Connell ................................................................................... 108
    Mike Kosgei ....................................................................................................... 111
    Coach Kiplimo of the Second Rifles Brigade ............................................... 114
    Coaches Albert Masai and Danny Kibet ...................................................... 115
    Kapsabet Coach Amos Korir ........................................................................... 117
800 and 1500 Meters ............................................................................................... 118
    Benson Koech .................................................................................................... 118
    Nixon Kiprotich ................................................................................................ 122
    William Tanui .................................................................................................... 125
    Kip Cheruiyot .................................................................................................... 127
    Japhet Kimutai .................................................................................................. 131
The Steeplechase ..................................................................................................... 135
    Patrick Sang ....................................................................................................... 137
    Charles Kwambai ............................................................................................. 144
5000 and 10,000 Meters .......................................................................................... 149
    Training for the 5000/10,000m ....................................................................... 149
    Lydia Cheromei ................................................................................................ 152
    Richard Chelimo ............................................................................................... 155
The Marathon ........................................................................................................... 161
    A Week of Michael Kapkiai's Marathon Training ...................................... 163
    Armed Forces Marathon Training ................................................................. 164
    Moses Tanui ...................................................................................................... 167
    Tegla Loroupe ................................................................................................... 172
    Cosmas Ndeti ................................................................................................... 175
Cross Country ........................................................................................................... 181
    John Ngugi ......................................................................................................... 184
    Paul Tergat ........................................................................................................ 188
    Rose Cheruiyot ................................................................................................. 193

# Foreword

In the mid-1960s, when Kenya emerged as a world power in track, Tropical Africa seemed an improbable place for distance runners to come from. For decades, athletes from the cool climes of Northern Europe—the British Isles, Scandinavia, the Soviet bloc—had dominated the distance events, now and then giving way to interlopers from North America or Down Under, or to North Africans running for France. But sub-Saharan Africa, as far as track fans were concerned, was still terra incognita—a land of future sprinters, perhaps, in that it was the ancestral home of so many American and Caribbean dashmen, but surely not distance runners.

Few recognized the portent in the marathon victory of Ethiopia's Abebe Bikila at the Rome Olympics in 1960. Eight years after that, though, there was no mistaking the significance of the nine medals East Africans won in the middle and long distance races at the Mexico City Games. The geographical center of distance running was shifting. It now lies almost exactly on the equator in a poor African country that for the first half of the century seemed no more likely a source of world class distance runners than, say, Gabon or Cameroon.

Why Kenya should have become the world's preeminent distance running nation is a complex question, but it's a little less mystifying if you keep in mind two general points about the country. First, although Kenya straddles the equator, its most populous regions don't fit anybody's stereotype of "tropical." More than three-quarters of the country's 28 million people live at altitudes of 5,000 feet or more, which means they enjoy a year-round climate that's something like summer in the former center of distance running, Northern Europe. What's more, of course, many of these high-altitude dwellers benefit from the thin air they breathe, developing powerful hearts and lungs to compensate for the deficiency of oxygen.

The second general point about Kenya is its state of economic development. By world standards, it's a poor country; the latest

*World Almanac* gives its per capita Gross Domestic Product as $1,170. The comparable figure for the U.S. is $27,607. Now poor countries, as a rule, are not sports powers; either their citizens are too busy scraping by to indulge in such frivolous pursuits, or the countries don't have the resources to support the institutions that organized sports require. Yet Kenya suffers neither of these crippling disadvantages. Why not?

First, Kenyans aren't quite so poor as the GDP numbers make them seem. Three-quarters of them are subsistence farmers who raise most of their own food and build their own homes out of materials that cost little or nothing, and since these activities don't figure into the cash economy, they are difficult to count in the GDP. In fact, compared to their fellow Africans, most Kenyans are quite well supplied with basic necessities. Malnutrition is rare, and while droughts produce occasional food shortages, famine is practically nonexistent. The infant mortality rate is among the lowest in Africa, life expectancy and literacy among the highest. More than 85% of all children attend at least a few years of primary school.

What accounts for Kenya's relative good fortune? In a sense, it comes back to altitude. The southwestern quarter of the country, where most of the population lives, is largely made up of highlands watered by moisture drifting over from massive Lake Victoria on Kenya's western border. It's some of the best farmland in Africa. This fact was not lost on the British when they built a railroad from the coast to the lake at the turn of the century. The aim was to secure the lake, the source of the Nile, for geopolitical purposes, but to help pay for the railroad, British authorities encouraged their countryman to settle in what soon became known as the White Highlands. The settlers, who had come to stay, built roads and bridges and towns and covered hillsides with huge plantations of coffee and tea—all, of course, with the help of minimally paid African labor on land forcibly expropriated from its original possessors.

Along with a modern economic infrastructure, the British introduced other familiar features of their own culture, including sport—golf, tennis, cricket, horse racing and polo for themselves; soccer, boxing and athletics (track and field) for the Africans. At first, African sport was concentrated in the army, the police and the country's few mission-run schools, but eventually British district officers were marking out running tracks on pasture land around the country and conducting regional meets that led to a Colony championship and sometimes an "inter-territorial" meet with neighboring Uganda. By the time of Independence in 1963, Kenya had sent small teams—mainly runners and boxers—to two Olympics and three Commonwealth Games.

After Independence, Kenyans took the base left them by the British and, well, ran with it. The government, as in many poor countries, was autocratic and corrupt, but it was also pro-West and relatively stable, so foreign investment poured in. And with increasing jet travel, tourists came in growing numbers to visit the country's magnificent game parks and Indian Ocean beaches. A sizable chunk of the government's proceeds from these enterprises went into education, especially at the secondary level, which had been largely neglected by the colonial administration. And with secondary schools came secondary school sports, a vital new avenue for athletic talent.

Before long, U.S. college coaches discovered this fresh source of educated, English-speaking athletes, and for a decade or two, until NCAA-imposed age restrictions made many Kenyans ineligible, hundreds of young men traveled to America to complete their education and develop their running skills. This exodus was decried at home, but it helped sustain Kenyan athletics through the disastrous Olympic boycotts of 1976 and 1980.

Then came the International Amateur Athletic Federation's liberalization of its oft-flouted amateur rules, and a few Kenyans began to earn serious money in Europe and the U.S. When the cash started filtering back to Kenya, it had a galvanizing effect on thousands of young men and women. They saw an opportunity to earn unimagined riches, and they began to train with the ferocious dedication that Toby Tanser documents so thoroughly in this book.

Now, having taken note of all this—relatively recent developments like scholarships and prize money, as well as Kenya's long-standing advantages, such as high altitude, a temperate climate, a reliable food supply and a solid athletic infrastructure—it's important to remember that Kenya is still a poor country. And interestingly, given the other circumstances, poverty, too, can be a plus when it comes to turning out hardy distance runners.

Consider the following points. First, houses in Kenya tend to be small, dark and smoky, and on average there's one TV set for every 106 people. This means that Kenyans, especially kids, spend most of their waking hours running around outdoors. Second, cars in Kenya are a luxury. There's one passenger car for every 180 people; the U.S. ratio is a hundred times greater—one car for every 1.8 people.

An obvious consequence of this disparity is that Kenyans cover a lot more ground on foot. Stories of kids running or walking several miles a day to school and back are by now tired clichés, but they're nonetheless significant. All those miles from early childhood—most of them, it should be noted, covered barefoot—can't fail to have helped condition young adult Kenyans to withstand training regimens that would injure legs unsteeled to such punishment.

Finally, in a country where the average income is roughly 4.2% of what it is in the U.S., it's hardly surprising that there's a great willingness to strive and sacrifice for the rewards available even to second- or third-rank distance runners. A net income of just $10,000 in a year is nearly nine times the average Kenyan's annual earnings.

So it seems that Kenya's altitude and its particular stage of economic development are a fortuitous combination that has helped to turn out legions of world class distance runners. The odd thing is that while the vast majority of Kenyans share these circumstances, the runners, with very few exceptions, have come from just four of the country's 40 tribes: the Kikuyu, the Kamba, the Kisii (or Gusii) and the Kalenjin. In fact, about three-fourths of Kenya's best runners come from just one of these tribes, the Kalenjin, who make up a little more than 10% of the population. To explore the reasons for this astonishing concentration of talent would take another book, but ethnic affiliation—and, sadly, friction—is such a central fact of Kenyan life (not unlike race in the U.S.) that it can't be ignored even in a book about training.

Tribal consciousness is pervasive, but acknowledging it is avoided in polite conversation. Kenyans rarely need to make explicit references to tribe in any case, since a person's name, accent or physiognomy will usually reveal his or her origins. If they want to make a point of ethnicity, Kenyans will often use a geographical euphemism in place of a tribal name, much as Americans use terms like "inner city." This sort of conversational delicacy is easy for Kenyans because the country's administrative regions have generally been drawn along tribal lines. Several of Kenya's 57 districts are actually named for their principal tribe or sub-tribe—the relevant examples here being Nandi District, Keiyo District, Marakwet District and Kisii District—and a few of the eight provinces (each of which encompasses several districts) are also closely identified with a particular tribe, so that referring to, say, Central Province, can be tantamount to speaking of the Kikuyu.

The trickiest of these multipurpose geographical terms is Rift Valley, and it requires some explanation here because it comes up frequently in the chapters that follow. Depending on the context, "Rift Valley" can mean any of several things: 1) The Rift Valley is a geological formation, a massive gash in the earth's crust that runs from the Dead Sea down through eastern Africa to Mozambique. It cuts right through Kenya, north-to-south, geologically splitting off the western third of the country. In its most populous part, it's about 30 miles wide, bordered on either side by steep escarpments that rise 2,000 feet or more. 2) Rift Valley Province is the largest of Kenya's administrative regions in both area and population. The province includes practically all of the actual valley, but it also takes in a great deal of territory on either side. 3) Rift Valley is increasingly used as a euphemism for the Kalenjin. Few Kalenjin live in the actual valley—most are spread out along its western rim and as much as 70 miles west of that—but the provincial boundary was drawn and redrawn, first by the British and later at the time of Independence, to include almost all of the tribe's territory. The Kalenjin now constitute close to half the province's population, and partly because the current president of Kenya, Daniel arap Moi, happens to be a member of the tribe, the Kalenjin are the politically dominant group in the province.

Finally, when a runner speaks of the Rift Valley as a place, he's generally referring neither to the actual valley nor to the province, but rather to the Kalenjin homeland, a region of rolling green hills and red dirt cow paths lying at altitudes of between 6,000 and 8,000 feet. And in these respects, the "Rift Valley" is quite similar to the homelands of two of Kenya's other running tribes, the Kisii and the Kikuyu. As you will see, all of these areas, Kenya's western highlands, constitute an ideal environment for the sort of training that has developed the corps of distance runners who now dominate the sport.

John Manners
February 1997

# Introduction

During the winter and spring, 1995-1996, I was privileged to experience a five-month vacation/training stint in Kenya. I was able to live among, train with and talk extensively with many of the country's leading runners and coaches. Upon my return to Europe, I was overcome by an immense sadness to have left that land. Almost all of the Kenyan people I met have a benevolent character all but lost now in Europe and America. The word *karibu* (welcome) had been ringing in my ears from the minute I arrived to the day I left.

The superstars of Kenyan athletics had been a great surprise. Used to the aloofness and me-first attitude of the typical European athletics "star," I was amazed by the helpfulness and hospitality of these remarkable African athletes. When I first met Paul Tergat, I wrote in my journal, "A man as warm as a winter stove." Patrick Sang and Moses Tanui deserve saintly status for their services to their countrymen. The immediate—and lasting—impression I had was of extraordinarily delightful human beings, and I thank them for a long, hot and pleasurable winter.

It was never my intention to write a book on the subject, but upon my return I was inundated with so many questions that I decided to write down some of the information I had gathered, photocopy the works and send it off to friends and fellow runners. The number of pages escalated and this book was born. The folks at Track & Field News agreed that the material I had accumulated was interesting and informative enough that it deserved wider exposure, given the fact that there is so much curiosity about Kenyan runners and their amazing accomplishments.

I hope the information presented here gives you some insight into their lifestyle and training. Their philosophies and training routines were startling to me, very different from the conventional approaches used elsewhere in the world. I try, in this book, to convey these differences to you. Many thanks to all the people of Kenya.

Toby Tanser
January, 1997

Tunisia

Morocco

Algeria

Senegal

Gambia

Nigeria

Ghana

Sudan

Ethiopia

Somalia

Uganda

Kenya

Burundi

Tanzania

Mozambique

**Kenya, its neighbors and the other significant track & field countries in Africa.**

Zambia

Zimbabwe

Namibia

South
Africa

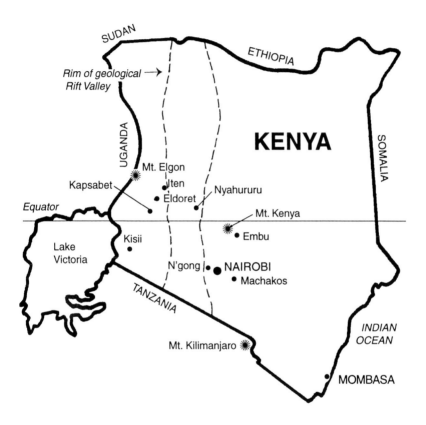

SUDAN

ETHIOPIA

Rim of geological → Rift Valley

UGANDA

**KENYA**

SOMALIA

Mt. Elgon

Kapsabet

Iten

Eldoret

Nyahururu

Equator

Mt. Kenya

Kisii

Embu

Lake
Victoria

N'gong

**NAIROBI**

Machakos

TANZANIA

INDIAN
OCEAN

Mt. Kilimanjaro

**MOMBASA**

A gallery of Kenyan stars from the 60s and 70s. Upper left: Henry Rono, setter of 5 world records and *Track & Field News* Athlete of the Year in 1978. Upper right: Ben Jipcho and Kip Keino, five world records and seven #1 rankings between them. Bottom left: Naftali Temu, Kenya's first Olympic champion. Bottom right: Wilson Kiprugut, Kenya's first Olympic medalist.

# Part 1
# Running in Kenya

# A Brilliant Record Of Success

## Kenyan Medalists In Major Championships Middle And Long Distance Events

### ■ OLYMPIC GAMES 1964-1996

No other country compares with Kenyan Olympic success in the men's middle and long distance events since 1968, even considering the fact that Kenya did not compete in the 1976 and 1980 Games. The total medal haul since 1968 is 12 gold, 14 silver, and 8 bronze in the six Olympics Kenya competed in 1968-1996, with at least one gold medal at each Games.

**1964 TOKYO** ........................................................................... **1 bronze**

| | |
|---|---|
| 800 | Bronze, Wilson Kiprugut 1:45.9 |
| | Kip Keino, 5th, 5000 |

**1968 MEXICO** ............................................... **3 gold, 3 silver, 1 bronze**

| | |
|---|---|
| 800 | Silver, Wilson Kiprugut 1:44.5 |
| 1500 | Gold, Kip Keino 3:34.9 |
| 3000 St | Gold, Amos Biwott 8:51.0; Silver, Benjamin Kogo 8:51.6 |
| 5000 | Silver, Kip Keino 14:05.2; Bronze, Naftali Temu 14:06.4 |
| 10,000 | Gold, Naftali Temu 29:27.4 |
| | Thomas Saisi, 7th, 800 |

**1972 MUNICH** ................................................. **1 gold, 2 silver, 1 bronze**

| | |
|---|---|
| 800 | Bronze, Mike Boit 1:46.0 |
| 1500 | Silver, Kip Keino 3:36.8 |
| 3000 St | Gold, Kip Keino 8:23.6; Silver, Ben Jipcho 8:24.6 |
| | Robert Ouko, 5th, 800; Mike Boit, 4th, 1500; Amos Biwott, 6th, 3000 St. |

## 1976 MONTREAL and 1980 MOSCOW

Kenya boycotted these Olympic Games.

## 1984 LOS ANGELES ...................................................... 1 gold, 1 bronze

| | |
|---|---|
| **10,000** | Bronze, Michael Musyoki 28:06.46 |
| **3000 St** | Gold, Julius Korir 8:11.80 |

Billy Konchellah, 4th, 800; Edwin Koech, 6th, 800;
Joseph Chesire, 4th, 1500; Julius Kariuki, 7th, 3000 St;
Paul Kipkoech, 5th, 5000; Charles Cheruiyot, 6th, 5000;
Sosthenes Bitok, 6th, 10,000; Joseph Nzau, 7th, Mar.

## 1988 SEOUL ............................................... 4 gold, 2 silver, 1 bronze

| | |
|---|---|
| **800** | Gold, Paul Ereng 1:43.45 |
| **1500** | Gold, Peter Rono 3:35.96 |
| **3000 St** | Gold, Julius Kariuki 8:05.51; Silver, Peter Koech 8:06.79 |
| **5000** | Gold, John Ngugi 13:11.70 |
| **10,000** | Bronze, Kipkemboi Kimeli 27:25.16 |
| **Mar** | Silver, Douglas Wakiihuri 2:10:47 |

Nixon Kiprotich, 8th, 800; Kip Cheruiyot, 7th, 1500;
Patrick Sang, 7th, 3000 St; Moses Tanui, 8th, 10,000.

"Our 'B' Team runners back home are just as good as the ones
we have brought here." Ibrahim Hussein, 1988 team captain.

## 1992 BARCELONA ............................................. 2 gold, 4 silver, 1 bronze

| | |
|---|---|
| **800** | Gold, William Tanui 1:43.66; Silver, Nixon Kiprotich 1:43.70 |
| **3000 St** | Gold, Matthew Birir 8:08.84; Silver, Patrick Sang 8:09.55; Bronze, William Mutwol 8:10.74 |
| **5000** | Silver, Paul Bitok 13:12.71 |
| **10,000** | Silver, Richard Chelimo 27:47.72 |

Joseph Chesire, 4th, 1500; Jonah Birir, 5th, 1500;
Yobes Ondieki, 5th, 5000; William Koech, 7th, 10,000;
Moses Tanui, 8th, 10,000.

A special award should go to Joseph Chesire. The five-time
Kenyan national 1500 champion (1985-89) placed fourth in three
major championship 1500s: Los Angeles 1984, Rome 1987 and
Barcelona 1992. At Seoul he was 11th in the 1500 final. Chesire,
an Eldoret resident, said, "I was very disappointed not to take
a medal, but it was a big achievement to make the Kenyan team

Olympic Champions: Upper left, Peter Rono, 1500m, 1988; upper right, Julius Kariuki, steeplechase, 1988; lower left, Paul Ereng, 800m, 1988; lower right, Julius Korir, steeplechase, 1984.

for three Olympics, and now it is time for my brother Mike." Joseph did win a bronze medal at the World Indoor Games in 1985.

**1996 ATLANTA ..............1 gold, 3 silver, 3 bronze + 1 silver (women)**

| | |
|---|---|
| **800** | Bronze, Fred Onyancha 1:42.79 |
| **1500** | Bronze, Stephen Kipkorir 3:36.72 |
| **3000 St** | Gold, Joseph Keter 8:07.12; Silver, Moses Kiptanui 8:08.33 |
| **5000** | Silver, Paul Bitok 13:08.16 |
| **10,000** | Silver, Paul Tergat 27:08.17 |
| **Mar** | Bronze, Eric Wainaina 2:12:44 |
| **W5000** | Silver, Pauline Konga 15:03.49 |

David Kiptoo, 6th, 800; Laban Rotich, 4th, 1500; William Tanui, 5th, 1500; Matthew Birir, 4th, 3000 St; Tom Nyariki, 5th, 5000; Josephat Machuka, 5th, 10,000; Paul Koech, 6th, 10,000; Rose Cheruiyot, 8th, W5000; Tegla Loroupe, 6th, W10,000.

Though Kenya took home only one gold medal, it was really a remarkable team performance in that the Kenyans claimed at least one medal in every men's event, 800 through the marathon. Their total medal tally in track & field placed Kenya third behind the American and Russian teams.

# ■ WORLD CHAMPIONSHIPS 1983-1995

After being shut out at Helsinki, Kenyan male middle and long distance runners have collected 12 gold medals, 6 silver, and 4 bronze—far and away the best record of any country in these events in the five World Championships 1983-1995.

### 1983 HELSINKI

No medals. Julius Korir was the best-placed Kenyan with a 7th place in the 3000 Steeplechase in 8:20.11. This essentially equaled Kenya's worst performance ever at a major international championship meet. (Nyandika Maiyoro was 7th in the 1956 Olympic 5000m for Kenya's only placing.)

**1987 ROME**................................................................**3 gold**

| | |
|---|---|
| **800** | Gold, Billy Konchellah 1:43.06 |
| **10,000** | Gold, Paul Kipkoech 27:38.63 |
| **Mar** | Gold, Douglas Wakiihuri 2:11:48 |

World Champions: Paul Kipkoech, upper left, won the 1987 10,000m. Kipkoech died in 1995 of cerebral malaria and tuberculosis. Billy Konchellah, above, won the 1987 and 1991 800m. Ismael Kirui, left, also won twice: the 1993 and 1995 5000m.

# WINNING IS EXPECTED

Winning medals at championship events are the important thing for the Kenyan athletics authorities. Only runners with realistic medal chances are sent. Joseph Ngure, coach of the national cross country team says, "It's a nice idea to take a large team, but there isn't the finance to support such a venture." This philosophy was never more apparent than in the 1996 World Junior Championships. The Kenyans won 10 medals with 19 athletes. In contrast, the U.S. won 12 medals with 110 athletes.

The glory Games for Kenya were the 1988 Olympics in Seoul—four gold medals. In 1996 at Atlanta, the Kenyan medal total was not helped by the absence of Daniel Komen. Komen, who later in the year became the overall Grand Prix winner, smashed both the two-mile and 3000m world records and defeated world record holder Haile Gebrselassie at Zurich— a week after the Games—by running the second fastest 5000 ever.

Though the team performed admirably in Atlanta, the reaction at home was one of failure, such is the expectation of the Kenyan public—only one gold medal was a disgrace! For example, look at these headlines from a Kenyan newspaper, *The Daily Nation:*

"Runners, Officials Let Kenyans Down"
"Wrong Attitude Did Kenyans In"
"Kenya's Image Suffers Major Blow In USA"
"Indiscipline Takes Its Toll."

And this account: "The triumphant national junior athletics team arrived in Nairobi from Sydney yesterday morning to a warm reception from government officials and family members. In sharp contrast to the cold reception accorded to the indisciplined Atlanta Olympic senior squad two weeks ago, the juniors were treated like royalty."

Obviously, the expectations were much too high even for a Kenyan dream team. In an article entitled, "The Atlanta Gold Mine," Kenya's second-largest newspaper, *The East African Standard*, predicted 1-2-3 sweeps in both the marathon and steeplechase, building the nation's hopes. The advance publicity and marketing in Kenya promised lots of gold medals and unprecedented success. "The Kenyan public does not understand that we are not unbeatable," commented William Tanui.

Stephen Ole Marai, 6th, 800; Joseph Chesire, 4th, 1500;
Peter Koech, 7th, 3000 St; Patrick Sang, 8th, 3000 St.

## 1991 TOKYO ..................................4 gold, 3 silver + 1 bronze (women)

| | |
|---|---|
| **800** | Gold, Billy Konchellah 1:43.99 |
| **1500** | Silver, Wilfred Kirochi 3:34.84 |
| **3000 St** | Gold, Moses Kiptanui 8:12.59; Silver, Patrick Sang 8:13.44 |
| **5000** | Gold, Yobes Ondieki 13:14.45 |
| **10,000** | Gold, Moses Tanui 27:38.74; Silver, Richard Chelimo 27:39.41 |
| **W3000** | Bronze, Susan Sirma 8:39.41 |

Paul Ereng, 4th, 800; David Kibet, 7th, 1500;
Julius Kariuki, 4th, 3000 St; Thomas Osano, 4th, 10,000;
Susan Sirma, 7th, W1500.

## 1993 STUTTGART ...... 3 gold, 2 silver, 2 bronze + 1 bronze (women)

| | |
|---|---|
| **800** | Gold, Paul Ruto 1:44.71; Bronze, Billy Konchellah 1:44.89 |
| **5000** | Gold, Ismael Kirui 13:02.75 |
| **3000 St** | Gold, Moses Kiptanui 8:06.36; Silver, Patrick Sang 8:07.53 |
| **10,000** | Silver, Moses Tanui 27:46.54; Bronze, Richard Chelimo 28:06.02 |
| **W10,000** | Bronze, Sally Barsosio 31:19.38 |

William Tanui, 7th, 800; Matthew Birir, 4th, 3000 St;
Paul Bitok, 8th, 5000; Boniface Merande, 7th,
Mar; Tegla Loroupe, 4th, W10,000.

## 1995 GÖTEBORG ........ 2 gold, 1 silver, 2 bronze + 1 bronze (women)

| | |
|---|---|
| **3000 St** | Gold, Moses Kiptanui 8:04.16; Silver, Christopher Kosgei 8:09.30 |
| **5000** | Gold, Ismael Kirui 13:16.77; Bronze, Shem Kororia 13:17.59 |
| **10,000** | Bronze, Paul Tergat 27:14.70 |
| **W10,000** | Bronze, Tegla Loroupe 31:17.66 |

Josephat Machuka, 5th, 10,000; Joseph Kimani, 6th,
10,000; Rose Cheruiyot, 7th, W5000.

## 1997 ATHENS ....................2 gold, 2 silver, 2 bronze + 1 gold (women)

| | |
|---|---|
| **3000 St** | Gold, Wilson Boit 8:05.84; Silver, Moses Kiptanui 8:06.04; Bronze, Bernard Barmasai 8:06.04 |
| **5000** | Gold, Daniel Komen 13:07.38; Bronze, Tom Nyariki 13:11.09 |

| 10,000 | Silver, Paul Tergat 27:25.62 |
| W10,000 | Gold, Sally Barsosio 31:32.92 |
| | Patrick Konchellah, 4th, 800; Patrick Ndururi, 7th, 800; Paul Koech, 4th, 10,000; Lydia Cheromei, 5th, W5000; Tegla Loroupe, 6th, W10,000. |

# ■ COMMONWEALTH GAMES 1966-1994

Another unrivaled record of success, 800 meters through the marathon, for the male Kenyan runners: 19 gold medals, 13 silver, and 10 bronze in the seven Commonwealth Games competed in since 1966.

## 1966 KINGSTON ..................................................... 3 gold, 1 silver, 1 bronze

| 800 | Silver, Wilson Kiprugut 1:47.2 |
| Mile | Gold, Kip Keino 3:55.3 |
| 3000 St | Bronze, Benjamin Kogo 8:33.2 |
| 3-Mile | Gold, Kip Keino 12:57.4 |
| 6-Mile | Gold, Naftali Temu 27:14.6 |

## 1970 EDINBURGH ........................................... 2 gold, 1 silver, 2 bronze

| 800 | Gold, Robert Ouko  1:46.8 |
| 1500 | Gold, Kip Keino 3:36.6 |
| 3000 St | Silver, Ben Jipcho 8:29.6; Bronze, Amos Biwott 8:30.8 |
| 5000 | Bronze, Kip Keino 13:27.6 |

## 1974 CHRISTCHURCH ... 3 gold, 1 silver, 3 bronze + 1 bronze (women)

| 800 | Gold, John Kipkurgat 1:43.9; Silver, Mike Boit 1:44.1 |
| 1500 | Bronze, Ben Jipcho 3:33.2 |
| 3000 St | Gold, Ben Jipcho 8:20.8; Bronze, Evans Mogaka 8:28.6 |
| 5000 | Gold, Ben Jipcho 13:44.4 |
| 10,000 | Bronze, Richard Juma 27:57.0 |
| W800 | Bronze, Sabina Chebichi 2:02.6 |

## 1978 EDMONTON ......... 3 gold, 3 silver, 2 bronze + 1 silver (women)

| 800 | Gold, Mike Boit 1:46.4; Bronze, Peter Lemashon 1:47.6 |
| 3000 St | Gold, Henry Rono 8:26.5; Silver, James Munyala 8:32.2; Bronze, Kiprotich Rono 8:34.1 |
| 5000 | Gold, Henry Rono 13:23.0; Silver, Michael Musyoki 13:29.9 |
| 10,000 | Silver, Michael Musyoki 28:19.1 |
| W 800 | Silver, Tecla Chemabwai 2:02.9 |

## 1982 BRISBANE ................................................. 1 gold, 1 silver, 2 bronze

| | |
|---|---|
| 800 | Silver, James Maina 1:45.48 |
| 1500 | Bronze, Mike Boit 3:43.33 |
| 3000 St | Gold, Julius Korir 8:23.94 |
| 5000 | Bronze, Peter Koech 13:36.95 |

## 1986 EDINBURGH

Kenya was one of 32 nations boycotting the 1986 Commonwealth Games

## 1990 AUCKLAND ................................................. 3 gold, 5 silver

| | |
|---|---|
| 800 | Gold, Sammy Tirop 1:45.98; Silver, Nixon Kiprotich 1:46.00 |
| 1500 | Silver, Wilfred Kirochi 3:34.41 |
| 3000 St | Gold, Julius Kariuki 8:20.64; Silver, Joshua Kipkemboi 8:24.26 |
| 5000 | Silver, John Ngugi 13:24.94 |
| 10,000 | Silver, Moses Tanui 28:11.56 |
| Mar | Gold, Douglas Wakiihuri 2:10:27 |

## 1994 VICTORIA ............................. 4 gold, 1 silver + 2 bronze (women)

| | |
|---|---|
| 800 | Gold, Patrick Konchellah 1:45.18 |
| 1500 | Gold, Reuben Chesang 3:36.70 |
| 3000 St | Gold, Johnstone Kipkoech 8:14.72; Silver, Gideon Chirchir 8:15.25 |
| 10,000 | Gold, Lameck Aguta 28:38.72 |
| W800 | Bronze, Gladys Wamuyu 2:03.12 |
| W10,000 | Bronze, Jane Omoro 32:13.01 |

# *IAAF World Cross Country Championships 1981-1997*

Kenyan world dominance in cross country running is even more astonishing. In the 12 years 1986-1997, Kenyan men failed to provide the individual senior men's champion only twice. From 1985-1997, Kenyan junior men provided the individual champion 9 out of 13 years. In the team scoring, Kenyan senior men have won the last 12 years (1986-1997) and never finished worse than 4th since their first participation in 1981. The senior women have won 5 of the last 7 years (1991-1997). The junior men have won the last 10 years (1988-1997) and the junior women 8 of the 9 years this event has been on the program. That's a total, for all divisions, of 35 team championships out of 49 in which they participated, including 24 individual champions.

## CHAMPIONS

**Senior Men**
1986—John Ngugi
1987—John Ngugi
1988—John Ngugi
1989—John Ngugi
1992—John Ngugi
1993—William Sigei
1994—William Sigei
1995—Paul Tergat
1996—Paul Tergat
1997—Paul Tergat

**Senior Women**
1994—Helen Chepngeno

**Junior Men**
1985—Kimeli Kipkemboi
1987—Wilfred Kirochi
1988—Wilfred Kirochi
1990—Kipyego Kororia
1992—Ismael Kirui
1993—Philip Mosima

1994—Philip Mosima
1996—David Chelule
1997—Elijah Korir

**Junior Women**
1991—Lydia Cheromei
1993—Gladys Ondeyo
1994—Sally Barsosio
1997—Rose Koskei

## TEAM SCORING  (place & points)

**Senior Men**
1981—3  (220)
1982—4  (271)
1983—3  (191)
1984—4  (233)
1985—2  (141)
1986—1  (45)
1987—1  (53)
1988—1  (23)
1989—1  (44)
1990—1  (42)
1991—1  (38)
1992—1  (46)
1993—1  (25)
1994—1  (34)
1995—1  (62)
1996—1  (33)
1997—1  (51)

**Senior Women**
1987—5  (117)
1988—6  (122)
1989—DNC
1990—12  (189)
1991—1  (36)
1992—1  (47)
1993—1  (52)
1994—3  (75)
1995—1  (26)
1996—1  (24)
1997—2  (34)

**Junior Men**
1985—2  (26)
1986—2  (32)
1987—2  (20)
1988—1  (13)
1989—1  (14)

1990—1  (12)
1991—1  (19)
1992—1  (18)
1993—1  (10)
1994—1  (18)
1995—1  (23)
1996—1  (13)
1997—1  (13)

**Junior Women**
1989—1  (40)
1990—1  (19)
1991—1  (18)
1992—3  (59)
1993—1  (10)
1994—1  (11)
1995—1  (18)
1996—1  (21)
1997—1  (15)

# Track & Field News #1 Rankings
## 1966-1996
## Men—800-Marathon

| | |
|---|---|
| 1966 | Kip Keino, 5000; Naftali Temu, 10,000. |
| 1967 | Naftali Temu, 10,000. |
| 1968 | Kip Keino, 1500; Amos Biwott, 3000 St. |
| 1970 | Kip Keino, 1500. |
| 1972 | Kip Keino, 3000 St. |
| 1973 | Ben Jipcho, 1500; Ben Jipcho, 3000 St. |
| 1974 | Ben Jipcho, 5000. |
| 1975 | Mike Boit, 800. |
| 1978 | Henry Rono, 3000 St; Henry Rono, 5000; Henry Rono, 10,000. |
| 1984 | Julius Korir, 3000 St. |
| 1987 | Billy Konchellah, 800; Paul Kipkoech, 10,000. |
| 1988 | Julius Kariuki, 3000 St; John Ngugi, 5000. |
| 1989 | Paul Ereng, 800; Peter Koech, 3000 St. |
| 1990 | William Tanui, 800; Julius Kariuki, 3000 St. |
| 1991 | Moses Kiptanui, 3000 St; Yobes Ondieki, 5000; Moses Tanui, 10,000. |
| 1992 | William Tanui, 800; Moses Kiptanui, 3000; Moses Kiptanui, 3000 St. |
| 1993 | Nixon Kiprotich, 800; Moses Kiptanui, 3000 St; Ismael Kirui, 5000; Yobes Ondieki, 10,000. |
| 1994 | Wilson Kipketer (now a Danish national), 800; Moses Kiptanui, 3000 St; William Sigei, 10,000. (Kipketer, running for Denmark, placed 1st in the 800m in 1995 and 1996, as well.) |
| 1995 | Moses Kiptanui, 3000; Moses Kiptanui, 3000 St. |
| 1996 | Daniel Komen, 3000; Joseph Keter, 3000 St; Daniel Komen, 5000. |
| 1997 | Moses Kiptanui, 3000 St; Sally Barsosio, W10,000. |

28 #1 rankings in 6 events in the last 11 years. Kiptanui leads Kenyans in #1 rankings with 8.

## Kenyan World Record Setters

| | |
|---|---|
| 3000 St | Ben Jipcho 8:20.8 (=WR), 1973; Ben Jipcho 8:19.8, 1973; Ben Jipcho 8:14.0, 1973; Henry Rono 8:05.4, 1978; Peter Koech 8:05.35, 1989; Moses Kiptanui 8:02.08, 1992; Moses Kiptanui |

7:59.18, 1995; Wilson Boit 7:59.08, 1997; Bernard Barmasai 7:55.72, 1997.

5000     Kip Keino 13:24.2, 1965; Henry Rono 13:08.4, 1978; Henry Rono 13:06.20, 1981; Moses Kiptanui 12:55.30, 1995; Daniel Komen 12:39.74, 1997.

10,000    Samson Kimobwa 27:30.5, 1977; Henry Rono 27:22.5, 1978; Richard Chelimo 27:07.91, 1993; Yobes Ondieki 26:58.38, 1993; William Sigei 26:52.23, 1994; Paul Tergat 26:27.85, 1997.

*Non-Olympic Events*

2 Miles    Moses Kiptanui 8:09.01, 1994; Daniel Komen 8:03.54, 1996; Daniel Komen 7:58.61, 1997.

3000     Kip Keino 7:39.6, 1965; Henry Rono 7:32.1, 1978; Moses Kiptanui 7:28.96, 1992; Daniel Komen 7:20.67, 1996.

Twenty-seven world records in five events, including the first runner under 27 minutes in the 10,000 (Ondieki), the first below 8 minutes in the steeplechase (Kiptanui), and the first under 8 minutes for 2 miles (Komen).

# *Boston Marathon*
## *Winners*

| 1988 | Ibrahim Hussein | 2:08:43 |
|------|-----------------|---------|
| 1991 | Ibrahim Hussein | 2:11:06 |
| 1992 | Ibrahim Hussein | 2:08:14 |
| 1993 | Cosmas Ndeti | 2:09:33 |
| 1994 | Cosmas Ndeti | 2:07:15 |
| 1995 | Cosmas Ndeti | 2:09:22 |
| 1996 | Moses Tanui | 2:09:16 |
| 1997 | Lameck Aguta | 2:10:34 |

VICTOR SAILER/PHOTO RUN

**Cosmas Ndeti won the Boston Marathon three times. Here's the finish of his first victory in 1993.**

## TOP TEN RANKINGS BY *TRACK & FIELD NEWS* OF KENYAN MEN, 800-MARATHON, FOR THE TEN YEARS 1988-1997

| Event | 1997 | 1996 | 1995 | 1994 | 1993 | 1992 | 1991 | 1990 | 1989 | 1988 | % of Placings |
|---|---|---|---|---|---|---|---|---|---|---|---|
| 800 | 2,3,10 | 4,6,7,10 | 3,5 | 1,2,4,7,9 | 1,3,4,5,6 | 1,2,8 | 2,4,5,7 | 1,2,8 | 1,3,7 | 3,9 | 34 of 100 (34%) |
| 1500 | 2,7,8,9 | 4,5,7,8 | 9 | 6,9 | 10 | 2,3,7,10 | 3,8 | 7 | 3,4,7 | 5,8 | 24 of 100 (24%) |
| 3000 | 2,4,5 | 1,3,4,5 | 1,8,10 | 3,4 | 3,5 | 1,2,3,5 | 5 | 3 | 2 |  | 21 of 45* (47%) |
| Steep | 1,2,3,4,5 6,7,8,10 | 1,2,3,4,5,6, 8,9,10 | 1,2,3,4,5,6, 7,9 | 1,2,3,5,7,8, 10 | 1,2,5,6,9 | 1,2,3,4,5,6 | 1,2,3,4,6,9 | 1,2,3,5,8 | 1,2,3 | 1,2,4 | 61 of 100 (61%) |
| 5000 | 2,4,5,9 | 1,7,8,9,10 | 2,3,7,8 | 10 | 1,4,6,8,9 | 2,3,4,8 | 1,6,7,8 | 4,5 | 4,6 | 1 | 32 of 100 (32%) |
| 10,000 | 2,3,9,10 | 3,4,5,6 | 3,5,7,8,9,10 | 1,4,5,9 | 1,4,5,6,7 | 2,8 | 1,2,4,5,7 | 5 | 4,6 | 3,9 | 35 of 100 (35%) |
| Mar | 4,8,9,10 | 4,6 | 4,6,9 | 3 | 5 | 9 | 8 | 2 | 3 | 6,9 | 17 of 100 (17%) |

*T&FN ranked only 1-5, 1989-1997, except for 1995 when 10 were ranked.

No other event in the track & field program is dominated by a single country as much as the Kenyans dominate the steeplechase. In the last 4 years, 33 of the 40 top ten places went to Kenyans (83%). They have placed 1-2 each year since 1988; 1-2-3 eight out of the last nine years; 1-2-3-4 five of the last seven. In the 800, Kenya has 5 #1 rankings in the last 10 years (and three of the other years the #1 ranking went to a transplanted Kenyan—Wilson Kipketer).

**Peter Koech broke the world record and ranked #1 in the steeplechase in 1989.**

# KENYANS IN THE 1997 *TRACK & FIELD NEWS* WORLD RANKINGS

**800**
2nd, Patrick Konchellah
3rd, Patrick Ndururi
10th, David Kiptoo
(#1, Wilson Kipketer of Denmark is a native Kenyan)

**1500**
2nd, Daniel Komen
7th, Laban Rotich
8th, William Tanui
9th, John Kibowen

**5000**
2nd, Daniel Komen
4th, Thomas Nyariki
5th, Paul Koech
9th, Paul Tergat

**10,000**
2nd, Paul Tergat
3rd, Paul Koech
9th, Dominic Kirui
10th, Elijah Korir

**3000 St**
1st, Moses Kiptanui
2nd, Wilson Boit
3rd, Bernard Barmasai
4th, Eliud Barngetuny

5th, Patrick Sang
6th, Joseph Keter
7th, John Kosgei
8th, Paul Kosgei
10th, Matthew Birir

**3000**
2nd, Daniel Komen
4th, Paul Bitok
5th, Thomas Nyariki

**W1500**
4th, Jackline Maranga

**MARATHON**
4th, John Kagwe
8th, Joseph Chebet
9th, Elijah Lagat
10th, Eric Kimaiyo

**W5000**
2nd, Lydia Cheromei
4th, Sally Barsosio

**W10,000**
1st, Sally Barsosio
7th, Tegla Loroupe

**W3000**
4th, Sally Barsosio

**W MARATHON**
2nd, Tegla Loroupe
6th, Joyce Chepchumba

**Daniel Komen**

**Moses Kiptanui**

*30*

# *Training Scenes*

*Believe. If you believe you can do it, you can.*

The Moi Air Base residential training camp came to life for the second time that day. A shrill whistle pierced the hot late morning air calling the runners, who had been relaxing for about $2^1/_2$ hours since their early morning run, to assemble before coach Danny Kibet.

Bodies dressed in an assortment of sun-bleached athletic attire drag their fatigued limbs toward Kibet, the resident camp coach, who stands stoically on the exit road.

"Is anybody suffering from injuries today?" he barks. There is stony silence from the gathering of 40-odd athletes. Apparently everyone is in fighting trim despite the protestations of aches and pains that had been bandied about by the breakfasting runners (or at least no one wished to own up to any weakness or fallibility). "Okay, then, I want an hour run. Start off easy, especially on the tarmac. You can speed up a bit when you reach the dirt road. Okay, then, off you go. Remember, easy at the start!" Kibet's words trail off as the large pack stumbles stiffly along the road at a pace barely above walking speed.

After the first corner is passed, the runners now feel the soft red dirt road underfoot and the pace quickly steps up to a steady but not uncomfortable pace. One runner bursts from the pack and opens up an instant gap of more than 50 meters. No one comments. No one follows.

The route now drops headlong into the basin of the Rift Valley, the heat intensifying as the runners descend. By the roadside children interrupt their games to watch the large contingent of runners who are beginning to pick up the pace. The breakaway leader boomerangs back to the assembly, which includes several world class runners.

Stride length increases due to the continuing descent and the tight formation of the pack begins to rupture. A giraffe cranes his neck around to check out the approaching multitude, then idly returns to the tree he is lunching on. A small boy clothed in black rags and dust sprints to try to join the pack—he manages about ten dancing strides before abandoning his moment of glory.

After 45 minutes, one of the leaders shouts out a command, causing the runners to skid to a halt and turn about. As they double back, the slower runners are rewarded with the opportunity to rejoin the pack. It doesn't take long for the pace to be restored to an intense level. Nearly everyone is breathing with burden, beads of sweat spraying like raindrops from the runners.

The hellish climb back up the seemingly vertical Rift Valley wall approaches. There is no respite in pace, no allowance for gradient. About half a dozen runners now govern the group, which although still in some contact is now well strung out.

Simon Chemoiywo, fresh from a sizzling performance in Brazil, is constantly pushing the boundaries of speed endurance. His expression is blank, his focus undivided. On his shoulder, stride for stride, there are others quite willing to take on the leadership role should the pace diminish an iota. The scarcity of oxygen at this altitude is now becoming severely apparent, as the runners battle against the incline and the heat.

Round each bend another steep grade appears, the summit hidden from view. Paul Tergat's face actually looks like he's enjoying himself. Perhaps he is the only one not laboring in breath and muscle fatigue.

Finally the road planes out and the military compound can be seen. The tempo gently cradles into comfortable speed as the runners float one by one into the encampment past Coach Kibet.

Afterward, some athletes do some stretching, others chat. No one has much interest in more energy-sapping exercises. Tea is made, hot and sweet, and all seek refreshment. For most of the runners, today's principal session was run at competition-level intensity—the prize being the chance to do it all again the following day!

Perhaps the hardships of life take away the comforts of dreams. The Kenyans I observed do not sit around waiting for a lucky break or a miraculous transformation of athletic form. They believe in the input equals output ratio.

"Hard training is our secret." Ismael Kirui echoes the feeling of most Kenyan athletes.

"Kenyans rely on training long hours and running over the hills," says Brother Colm O'Connell of St. Patrick's School, a renowned athletic power among Kenyan secondary schools.

"I was so happy to see my cousin [Susan Sirma] doing well and earning good money. I said to myself, 'One day I must be like her,'" spoke Sally Barsosio, explaining why she had begun hard training.

These runners simply believe that through hard training they will succeed at the highest of levels. William Kiprono, who has yet to travel outside Kenya, has been training and racing for many years. Despite winning the Army steeplechase and finishing second in the 10,000m on consecutive days in 1996 (against such notable runners as William Mutwol and Ondoro Osoro), he remains optimistic, hoping that one day he'll get a passport and a plane ticket to Europe. "I know I will win if I race in Europe," William says with an almost religious conviction. Year after year, teams are selected and he has remained behind. When asked why, against the odds, he continues to train, William answers, "I know I will make it with hard training."

Brother Colm points this out as a major factor. "They run hard because they love to run hard; they enjoy the practice and have great levels of perseverance. Life itself is hard in Kenya." The possibility of financial reward and a ticket to Europe is definitely on their minds, but without the enjoyment and ability to endure long, hard training, there wouldn't be anything close to the legions of runners Kenya has supplied to the highest levels of world distance running.

## *Training In The Schools*

Four of the most successful secondary schools—athletics-wise—are St. Patrick's, Singore, Kipsoen and Kapkenda. Each of the four is a boarding school. (These students, therefore, do not run a dozen miles to school, contrary to what westerners have been led to believe.)

Physical exercise in Kenyan secondary schools is seen as an important factor in a child's upbringing. Thirty kilometers from Eldoret, there is a small girls' high school. Singore Girls' is home to some 400 boarding students. Each afternoon one hour is set aside for sport and conditioning. Hockey, running, and basketball are three sports commonly practiced. On Sunday, the girls are free to do as they like, but most of them choose to spend an hour at their favorite sport. When I visited, a group of girls who had planned a basketball game began by warming up with 20 minutes of vigorous running at various tempos before taking to the court—a sure sign of good teaching and a natural love for exercise!

Shortly after 6:00am each morning a group of girls leave the school's gates for a morning training run, many barefoot or fitted with "everyday" shoes. They return before 7:00 to wash and eat breakfast before the day's regular schedule begins.

This "system" has produced astonishing results. In 1991, four girls from this school placed 1, 2, 6, and 9 at the World Cross Country Championships (Junior Women), capturing the team title. Sally Barsosio who won the World Junior X-C title in 1994 is Singore's latest prodigy. As you've seen from the statistical chapter, Kenyan junior women have won the world team title seven out of the eight years since this Championships division was introduced, so it's not just Singore Girls' School that is turning out outstanding runners.

The schools in Kenya are well aware of the potential rewards and prestige involved in running. Running training is encouraged. At Kipsoen Secondary School, the girls who are training have their own dormitory. Nancy Kiprop, 4th at the 1996 World X-C Championships (3rd in 1995), points out the advantages. "We are not disturbed here, and we don't disturb others when we rise early for our training each day before school hours." Roommate and fellow World X-C medalist Jebiwott Keitany is quick to add that they receive no special privileges, with no special leniency for time away from studies. "If we are late to classes, we will be punished like any other student." The young athletes motivate each other and are all present at each morning's run. Advised by Brother Colm, the girls train twice a day, before and after school hours. Tempo runs and hill repeats are on the menu for nearly every day.

The runners at St. Patrick's High School have it a little easier, according to Martin Pepela, a student in form three. "Kwambai (one of the school's top runners) doesn't come to a lot of our lectures. He is usually relaxing, staying in bed." (Charles Kwambai eventually left school without graduating in part because of his unwillingness to comply with the common school rules.)

The headmaster of St. Patrick's, Elijah Komen, is very proud of his runners. "The name of St. Patrick's is known throughout the world as the finest running school." In the 1995 African Junior Championships, St. Patrick's students, Kwambai and Japhet Kimutai, captured gold medals at all distances, 800m-10,000m, and their schoolmates took most of the silverware as well! The school record book is more like that of a large nation, not of a school in a small village. Take, for instance, 1:44 in the 800m! "At one time we had four sub-four-minute milers at the school at the same time," proudly smiles Brother Colm. Only three high schoolers in the U.S. have ever broken four minutes for the mile, the last

Left, 1988 Olympic 1500m champion Peter Rono standing by a Nandi flame tree planted in his honor at St. Patrick's school. Above, Charles Kwambai in St. Patrick's uniform. Below, distance runners Rose Cheruiyot, Florence Barsosio, and Lydia Cheromei Kogo relax by the gates of St. Patrick's. Photos by the author.

coming 30(!) years ago. This is not just dominance—it's another planet!

Growing in the central square of the St. Patrick's High School grounds is a thriving Nandi flame tree, planted in honor of Peter Rono's Olympic victory in the 1988 Olympic 1500. Just a couple of meters away is the "Birir bush," another Olympic gold medal commemoration (Matthew Birir, 1992 Olympic steeplechase). All students regularly pass this small garden of intentional inspiration. "So many great runners have been to this school—when you train with the runners of this school then you know that with hard work, you too can become a champion. Being at this school, you know it is possible," says one of the school's current middle distance stars.

It's not just the secondary schools that are infused with a running ethic. As part of the induction course into the Tambach Teachers Training College, all students must be involved in a period of running training. "One of the days we had to run up and down a steep hill. It was very hard, as I hadn't run for many, many years," recalled one student. Running is indeed a part of growing up in Kenya.

## The Ups And Downs Of Hard Training

The typical running training in Kenya does not suit everyone. There are many runners who find the work load too hard to handle. Coach Elijah Langat of the Air Force says, "You have to be invited to join the military training camps. Sometimes runners come and after a few days of our training, they sneak out and go home in the night, finding it too tough."

There is no idle chatter or fooling around during the training sessions. All the effort and concentration is geared toward running. Even at modest speeds, silence and seriousness are the norm.

Some Westerners believe that the Kenyans train too hard. The proof, they think, can be seen in the fact that Kenyans only last a season or two on the elite world circuit, with new runners quickly replacing the old.

I don't believe it's quite this simple, however. There are so many good runners in Kenya that it is definitely a problem to remain at the top. It's rare that one athlete will win a series of races in Kenya; it is much more common to have fluctuating results, because of the incredibly high quality of the competition. That's one reason sometimes elite runners do not perform well at a national trials competition and are left off the team (Daniel

Komen in 1996 is a case in point).

Take also the case of John Ngugi. Although a five-time World Cross Country champion and a 1988 Olympic gold medalist, Ngugi never won a major Kenyan competition after 1987. One year he was 76th in the national X-C championships prior to his winning the world championship. He wouldn't have made it out of Kenya that year if it hadn't been for his legendary status.

Ismael Kirui could not make the podium at the Armed Forces Championships in the 5000 in 1995 and just scraped onto the national team for that year's World Championships, which he won.

To succeed in Kenyan athletics is incredibly tough. To remain at the top takes superhuman efforts.

"They complained that we were training too hard. Kenyans would never complain." So spoke the great Moses Kiptanui about a group from the British national squad who went to train in Kenya. Kiptanui, the world's first and only sub-eight-minute steeplechaser, leads a training group in Nyahururu. Among his athletes is Daniel Komen, who broke the world 2-mile and 3000m records in 1996.

Nowadays, Kiptanui trains three times a day—an early-morning run of about 40 minutes at 6:00am; a quality session, often intervals, at 10:00am, and a long easy run in late afternoon. The Britons, however, should have visited a couple of years earlier when the amazing Kiptanui was logging four sessions a day. "I got up early and ran 10km, then before lunch I ran intervals on the track. In the afternoon there was hill training and in the evening a distance run."

It's not too much of an exaggeration to say that the effort many Kenyan athletes put in daily is similar to a week's worth of effort expenditure for the average American or European club runner.

Throughout the year various competitions are organized around the country. It is not uncommon to see a world champion trailing the field. Kenyan athletes at home use competitions differently than do Westerners.

Prizes for competitions are usually of little value, so races are seen more as means to test fitness and progress. Ismael Kirui, after finishing third in a small 10km race (29:46) explains, "Today was just speedwork, that's all." Kirui echoes the thoughts of his brother, Richard Chelimo, that in the training period, you train. Placement in races is unimportant.

The race completion percentage must be among the lowest in the world. Many Kenyans test themselves by starting at full speed, regardless of distance, dropping out as they reach exhaustion.

# The Varieties of Training

## In-Season Training

Once the period of hard base training is over the great migration begins—the Kenyans hit the racing scene all over the world. Often the work load is reduced. Richard Chelimo, after arriving Europe, would run intervals reduced in both quantity and quality. "Once you have the form it is very easy to ruin the shape with too much training." says Chelimo. Benson Koech is very careful to monitor his form. "If you train too hard then the season can be ruined; you must rest and begin the buildup again." Wilson Musto trains in Kenya for a few months then flies over to Germany when he feels in form. When in Europe he races most weekends and runs just one session per week. An example of Musto's in-season routine from the 1996 campaign is shown below:

| | | |
|---|---|---|
| April 18 | 67 mins easy jogging |
| | 19 | 57 mins easy jogging |
| | 20 | Travel to Holland |
| | 21 | 40 mins easy |
| | 22 | 60 mins easy |
| | 23 | 51 mins easy with some sprints |
| | 24 | Same as the 23rd |
| | 25 | 52 mins easy, 6x100m sprints |
| | 26 | 44 mins easy |
| | 27 | Rest day |
| | 28 | Rotterdam Marathon. Pacemaker till 30km, with splits of 10k—30.27, 15k—45.28, 21.1k—65.27 + 30k—1.32.57 |
| | 29 | Rest |
| | 30 | 60 mins easy |
| May 1 | 45mins easy |
| | 2 | 56 mins easy |

3   Travel to Sweden, 46 mins easy
4   47 mins easy
5   Cross country race, 2nd. "Still tired from Rotterdam!"
6   43 mins easy/46 mins normal
7   45 mins normal/45 mins normal

# Interval Training

Despite running fewer sessions, intervals or otherwise, on a conventional running track than most international elite runners, the Kenyan men are world leaders on the track, 800m to 10,000m. The World's top ten performer list for 1996 demonstrates the fact:

| | |
|---|---|
| 800m | 50% Kenyans |
| 1500m | 60% Kenyans |
| 3000m | 50% Kenyans (100% top five!) |
| Steeplechase | 90% Kenyans |
| 5000m | 50% Kenyans |
| 10,000m | 60% Kenyans |

Formatted interval sessions are usually embarked upon after the cross country season is over, in April. Many of the rural runners do not run intervals at all. However most of the runners in organized training groups, or in areas densely populated with runners, do run intervals. For the middle distance runner the distances are usually between 400m and 2000m. The number of repetitions are rarely decided until the day of training; even then the runner often will add more repeats if he feels the body has not been sufficiently exhausted.

A typical session for the Armed Forces would be 20 x 400m run at goal pace of 60-61 seconds with a 200m jog rest. The marathon runners would increase the amount of repeats, aiming for a 12km total of intervals, and slightly slow the tempo by a second or two. A typical session will see a lot of runners burning themselves out in the first few intervals and barely running the last few. Some appear to attack the session with no forethought as to self-preservation, especially the runners who have not made it onto the international circuit.

Mark Wendot Yatich has a typical approach. "I ran three times a day every day except on Sundays. I never ran intervals, just fast runs and steady runs. After winning a road race I came to the Air Force training camp. It was only then when I began with other kinds of training." This simple holistic attitude is perhaps one of the Kenyans' greatest assets, along with the ability to push their bodies past pain barriers close to exhaustion.

"Interval training is not always necessary in Kenya, as the runners reach the same intensity of work when out on a tempo distance run," noted Navy coach Danny Kibet. "You could go to the track at 10 o'clock in the morning and [Peter] Koech would be there running intervals; three hours later he would still be doing them. When he got too tired he'd temporarily rest at the side of the track before resuming. This could go on for hours!"

Intervals often are run on the red dirt roads of the Kenyan countryside. There are not many athletic tracks around the land, but this does not stop the Kenyans from being the world's best middle/long distance track runners! The tracks that are available are usually comparable to cowfields in smoothness and surfaced with cinders. "Intervals on the dirt roads help build up immense strength, " positively notes coach Mike Kosgei. "After running intervals on the tracks of Kenya I know I can fly round the tracks in Europe," points out Richard Chelimo.

The 70s style of interval running seems to be the most popular form in Kenya, the runners recording huge amounts of intervals, working the rest period with a short jog. Moses Kiptanui, along with Yobes Ondieki, are famed in Kenya for their tough interval sessions. "Yobes could go out in the morning and run a hard track session, then run another hard track session in the afternoon!" remembers Patrick Sang. "Moses trains similarly; I had to take a week's rest after training with him!"

Spending an hour or more continually running intervals was not uncommon for these runners. Kirwa Tanui, an 8:20+ altitude steeplechaser explains. "Sometimes when we are training in a group no one wants to say this is the last interval, so we all wait for each other. Consequently the session goes on and on!"

Often if an athlete feels that he has "hit" form on Kenyan soil he will reduce the intervals and concentrate on steady runs of around 60 minutes in the forest instead. "Peaking is an art; that is where we can help," says Coach Albert Masai of the Navy team. "The intervals must be planned, reducing in quantity as the main race period arrives." Here is a typical middle distance schedule the week before the Armed Forces Track Championships, the major event for the armed forces men:

| | |
|---|---|
| Sat | 6am Easy 40 mins jog |
| | 10am Long intervals, 8 x 800m. Full recovery, run at 5000m race pace |
| Sun | Rest day |

| Mon  | 6am Easy 40 mins jog |
|------|---------------------|
|      | 10am 40 mins steady run in the forest |
| Tue  | 6am Easy 40-60 mins |
|      | 10am 5 x 400m, sub 60 secs, with 1 min jog rest (a light session for the Kenyans!) |
| Wed  | 6am Easy 40 mins |
|      | 10am cross country run over one hour, steady tempo |
| Thur | 6am Easy 40 mins |
|      | 10am Light 200m intervals, "stretching the legs!" |
| Fri  | 6am 40 mins "easy, easy!" |
|      | Travel to competition |
| Sat  | Race day |

Note just two sessions per day at the most! Kenyans DO taper! Of course extra stretching and relaxing figure highly in the final days.

# Tempo Training

*"If I feel good then I run fast no matter what the session. Don't waste good time—if you feel good then run hard!" John "King of the Country" Ngugi.*

Tempo training is by far the most popular form of training in Kenya—runs of between 45 and 70 minutes run at speeds which mirror their racing efforts. Before many of the tempo runs the coaches will ask the runners to run at a predetermined pace: steady, moderately fast, or flat-out. However after 20 minutes there is usually someone who starts to push the pace, then another who wants to lead. Inevitably 90% of group training turns out to be a mini-competition at top speed. Even when a hard competition is within the next couple of days the runners seem unable to contain their natural competitive streak. As the runners fly back to the camp at speeds blatantly contradicting the coaches' wishes there are never reprimands, quite the opposite! The reasoning is explained by sub-28 10,000m runner Julius Ondieki. "Tempo running is practicing the pain we will face in competition; who wants to run slow in competition?"

As many as five sessions of this type of training are undertaken during the week. A common form of tempo running is that the runners start off fairly slowly, picking up the pace until the "halfway" mark when the run becomes full-speed-ahead. As the runners typically are running in a good-sized group, the pace never drops; each runner serves a spell at the front of the pack and pushes a little before the next takes over, not unlike cycling races. Simeon Rono, a member of the national cross country squad, points out that runners rarely win race after race because when a runner wins a race in Kenya he is usually training in one of the aforementioned groups. Thus the other runners know they can stay with his pace. Back to the "belief" theme again.

The tempo runs tend to be over hilly routes, often with a speed injection at the start of the hill, underlying the competitiveness of the session. The red dirt roads provide a forgiving surface that allows the legs to cope with the endless miles. The tempo session is also undertaken by injured athletes. Whereas a runner may rest from an interval session, or a hill run, most of the runners participate in the tempo run. "You can begin slowly and in a little pain and as the pace heats up the hurting disappears as you concentrate on keeping up," says Haron Kerio of the Air Force team.

Interestingly enough the runners who are often in the fore-front of the pack on such training runs are more often than not the "new" Kenyans to break through. This was true of Chelimo, Kirui and Tergat. This form of training brings out the best in the strong individual runner but can be a nightmare to the untrained or out-of-form athlete, though it will soon bring them back to form. "Runners in Europe were surprised how quickly I came back into form after a long injury time. This kind of training [tempo] really pulls you back into shape. There are no races in Europe as hard as the tempo runs here!" half jokes Julius Korir.

Fartlek is also a very popular system of training in Kenya. The reflection of the philosophy to push hard when feeling strong brings out the strengths of fartlek. A fartlek run can be turned into a tempo run if the runner is so inclined—this kind of improvisation suits the Kenyans. Structural fartlek, as a session of two minutes hard with one minute steady for 10km, are likewise used. William Sigei employs this method. In the training camps fartlek is utilized as a transition from cross country to track training.

# The Long Run

Most runners from the middle distances upward do a long run once a week. The distance covered varies greatly. Benson Koech, a middle distance man, may cover 20km and Michael

Kapkiai, a marathoner, up to four hours. The speeds also vary. Some believe in fast-paced distance, others in slow. Moses Tanui likes to run his distance at a steady pace with a fast five kilometers to finish off the run. Partrick Sang likes to run at an honest tempo from start to finish. The Armed Forces long runs often begin a at pleasant rambling pace only to end up like a cavalry charge—all-out to the finish.

It is very rare to see Kenyans drinking on their long runs. They generally wait till the conclusion of the run before hydrating with Kenyan *chai* (tea). Due to the relatively low humidity the runner does not lose as much fluid as, say, in New York at similar temperature.

Distances are irrelevant. The Kenyans run chiefly for time. The rural terrain typical of the Rift Valley is quite suited to prolonging or curtailing training sessions. During one training run in his hometown, Kirwa Tanui was asked how much further distance had to be covered before the training run was completed. "Oh, about two kilometers," smiled the steeplechaser. After 15 more minutes of strongly paced running Kirwa was again queried. "About two kilometers!" was the sincere reply.

| Athlete | Approximate Time of Long Run |
|---|---|
| Rose Cheruiyot | One hour |
| Paul Tergat | Up to one hour and thirty minutes |
| Moses Tanui | Two hours fifteen minutes |
| Michael Kapkiai | Over three hours. |

# Hill Work

The Kenyans lay great faith in hill work. To this Westerner's eyes, they appear to float rather than labor uphill with the greatest of ease and grace.

Much of Kenya's highlands is, of course, very hilly. On any training run, more likely than not one will encounter a few hills. These hills can ascend for miles and miles. Mix in the thin air and the heat and one gets a demanding session! In the organized training groups, there is usually a hill session once a week or more. These tend to vary between the short interval type, where the runners will run up and down the same hill a number of times, or the long drag, a hill which can be up to 25km long.

Mike Kosgei, the former national coach, favors a very steep 200m hill, with a dirt surface to allow the runner to drive hard up the hill. "I like the seniors to run at least 25 repeats, the juniors 20 times, the women 20 and the girls 15. When they reach the top there is no rest; turn and stride back down for the next repeat. This is a very tough session and the athlete should be rested before attempting it."

The Armed Forces camp uses a mountainside, the route taking 27 minutes to climb when run at a good clip. The cross country runners ascend once, the marathoners return for a second effort. Moses Tanui twice a week drives to a gravel road where he starts his hill session at 1300m altitude. The road relentlessly winds upwards to 2700m in 22 kilometers. Tanui runs solo up this hill with his Toyata Landcruiser driven behind him. "It takes around 1 hour, 30 minutes."

Up in the Nandi Hills near Kapsabet is a long winding tarmac road over a similar distance. Here Patrick Sang returns each year a few times to fine-tune his winter buildup. "All the greats have run this hill. Ibrahim Hussein often ran up this hill; his house is at the top. Kip Keino used to run here and Henry Rono ran his long run up this hill," remembered Sang's driver, a former national runner himself.

# *Rest And Recovery*

A major topic among running coaches is how to successfully balance recovery and hard training. Some athletes, Rob de Castella, for instance, trained year-round; others, such as Steve Ovett, took a yearly break from training.

The Kenyan system works very much around the circle of resting the body, building up, racing and resting again. It is not uncommon for athletes to take breaks up to three months or longer each year. Nearly every Kenyan athlete rests starting the month of October, with most not resuming training until December or January. Moses Kiptanui, who trains at superhuman intensities, always takes a two-month break after the season to recharge his batteries. 800m runner Nixon Kiprotich takes this opportunity to relax, put on a few pounds and catch up on the family life he has missed spending the summer on the European circuit. Patrick Sang takes the time for a family holiday before burying himself in the businesses he has been forced to neglect while abroad.

Be it just relaxing, business or family this break is important to the athletes. Chelimo explains, "Training is all time-consum-

World record setters in the 10,000m. Left, Samson Kimobwa was the first Kenyan to hold the WR in the 10,000m (1977). Yobes Ondieki, above, was the first runner under 27 minutes in this event (1993).

ing to us; when we train it takes all our time, a very intense period. Then we go over to Europe traveling from race to race. When we return to Kenya we need to get back the energy." Cosmas Ndeti is another athlete who believes in taking long breaks. "The marathon recovery can not be hurried; I like to eat well and spend time with my children, then begin a hard buildup."

Resuming full training the athletes seem to return to form with incredible ease and speed. Benson Koech began training in January 1996 after his yearly three-month break. He arrived in Iten with a sore leg after a public transport accident at the end of December. On February 3rd his manager contacted Benson with the offer of a series of indoor races, and on the 4th Benson heard there was a flight to Germany that evening for him. He then drove more than 300km to the airport, took a night flight and the next day he finished third, half a second behind Wilson Kipketer, running 2:18:40 for 1000 meters. Here is the training Benson used after his three-month layoff to bring him back to such form. As can be seen, rest plays a major role.

Altitude 2400m. Dirt track. January 1996.

| Day 3 | AM | 9.3km, 36 min. |
|---|---|---|
| Day 4 | AM | 7.7km, 30 min. |
| | MID | 6km, 28 min. |
| Day 5 | AM | 12km, 44 min. |
| | MID | Rest. |
| | PM | 7.7km, 29 min. |
| Day 6 | AM | 9.3km, 40 min. Travel home, rest. |
| Day 7 | | Rest. |
| Day 8 | | Transport wheat to Eldoret, no running. |
| Day 9 | AM | Rest. |
| | MID | 11km, 46 min. |
| | PM | 7.7km, 33 min. |
| Day 10 | AM | 9.3km, 36 min. |
| | MID | Travel to Eldoret. |
| | PM | 7.7km, 22 min. |
| Day 11 | AM | 11km, 35.28 min. |
| Day 12 | AM | Rest. |
| | PM | 8km, 33 min. |
| Day 13 | AM | Rest. |
| | MID | 11.7km, 41 min. |
| | PM | Travel home. |
| Day 14 | AM | Rest. |
| Day 15 | PM | 7.7km, 29 min. |
| Day 16 | AM | 12km, 41 min. |
| | MID | 10x200m, 5 min rest (25, 27, 25, 26, 26, 26, 26, 25, 27 + 25). |
| Day 17 | AM | 12km, 41 min. |
| | MID | 10x100m, 3 min rest (12, 13, 13, 13, 11, 12, 11, 12, 11, 12) + 2x150m (17 + 17). |

| Day 18 | | Rest. |
|--------|-----|------|
| Day 19 | AM | 12km, 41 min. |
| | MID | 5x300m, 5 min rest (40, 41, 42, 41 + 41) |
| Day 20 | AM | Rest. |
| | MID | 4x400m (57, 57, 55 + 56). |

# Rest During The Hard Training Period

Frequently a session of jogging is called upon, perhaps after an extra-harrowing morning interval session or long run. When the runners have decided upon a jog, then the speed is quite slow—8 or 9 minutes per mile is usual jogging pace. Although at this pace the athletes could easily converse without raising the pulse, they jog in stony silence. "Training is training; talking is for after the training," explained Christopher Kosgei. Another example of the intense focus Kenyans train with.

Rest during the week is usually scheduled for Sunday. Many of the Kenyan athletes are deeply religious and attend church services on this day. Life at the Armed Forces camp on such a day is very tranquil. Many runners take the opportunity to stay in bed late; those who don't walk down to the local church stay in camp reading the newspaper, writing home or taking a stroll. Some athletes do train and omit a weekly rest day; these are in the minority and they usually take an easy session on this day.

Before competitions runners often jog easily the morning of the day preceding the race. A light session of 40 minutes was found to be normal. If the race is an important competition, then the day after the race is also taken as a rest day to ensure full recovery. Paul Tergat takes a rest day after a competition, then two days of easy running before resuming his normal training schedule. Often the more established the athlete the more rest taken.

A team of the Second Army Brigade were to compete in the Iten cross country relays scheduled to start at 10:00am. At 6am two members of the four-man team who are still trying to make an international breakthrough, Kiprono and Kosgei, were out running 40 minutes of intense hill work. Kiprono was later to record the day's fastest leg!

An interesting concept used by a large majority of the Kenyan athletes is the employment of two training runs, both in the morning. By beginning the day's running schedule at 6am and finishing at roughly 11am, the athletes are giving their bodies a much longer time to recover than the full-time athlete who conventionally trains once in the morning and once in the afternoon. Whether the two-a-morning regimen is superior or not, one thing for sure is it works for the Kenyans!

# Strength Training

At Nyayo Stadium in Nairobi there is in actual fact a weight room. Some runners lift weights, sprinters mainly, but a few distance runners do lift on an irregular basis. Gyms are as rare as hen's teeth in Kenya, however. Instead the runners use forms of light exercise to gain strength, along with the actual running training which many argue is the best form of strength training. The Armed Forces have some homemade forms of strength equipment, as has Brother Colm O'Connell in Iten. Dumbbells made out of cement-filled paint cans joined by iron bars can be found. Looking at the arm musculature of most of the runners, however, these are not frequently used. When a session of ten press-ups was called for before one training run, large groans were heard and more than seven in ten failed to complete the set. The strength of the Kenyans is certainly not in their arms. Not one of ten subjects managed more than two pull-ups!

Farm chores, such as plowing or hauling sacks of seed, are undertaken by most athletes a couple of times a year. This work, which is performed generally without motorized machinery, is extremely rigorous and can take a week or more. It helps to maintain overall body strength.

Before training, and after a warm-up jog, the runners often indulge in light calisthenics. This is repeated also after the hard running session and the jog cool-down. One member of the group acts as supervisor and calls out a stretch or an exercise, then another runner comes up with a different one. The group follows along and the coaches prowl looking for anyone not putting in a good effort or stretching incorrectly. After a few of the exercises the body begins to feel as though an interval session has been run!

William Tanui ran through a few of his stock favorites with the ease and grace of an aerobics teacher. "It is very important to have a flexible and strong body; this we get from these exercises. The stride becomes much more efficient with these movements."

There is often laughter among the athletes in these sessions and a playful aspect that highlights the joy the Kenyans seem to derive from community and simple exercise. After about 20 different exercises and stretches the group will either stand up and begin the running session or walk off and be glad to complete another day's training. Sometimes an exercise session will replace running altogether. This was the case if the runner had trained twice before midday, then if the athlete was not feeling up for another run in the afternoon, a session of exercises was substituted. "Doing something is better than nothing!" says Kip Cheruiyot.

Below is a selection of the exercises and stretches commonly used. The stretch is usually held for between 10 and 20 seconds. The exercise repeats are individual for each exercise.

1. Hurdles, 10 each leg.
2. Pulling air, 10 secs each position.
3. Trunk bend, 45 secs, moving continuously side-front-side-front-back, etc.
4. Bent-knee bends, 20.
5. Leg hold-up, 20 secs each leg.
6. Slow trunk bend, hold the position 20 secs each foot.
7. The stance, hold 20 secs, then increase distance between the feet. Repeat 3 times.
8. Sit-ups, 10-15 times.
9. Press-ups, 10 times.
10. Quad stretch, hold 20 secs and move head to the knee.
11. Rotating hips, 10 times clockwise and 10 times anti-clockwise.
12. Turnbacks, fast movements.
13. Sitting toe touch, hold 30 secs. 20-30 times.
14. One-knee sit-ups.
15. Leg hovers, 10 secs in each position.
16. Knee lifts, 1 minute rigorous.
17. Standing start, 30 times as fast as possible, movement arms + legs, with the legs coming as far forward as possible.

## *Personal Themes*

| | |
|---|---|
| Daniel Komen | "Have patience; it takes years of hard training to get good results." |
| William Tanui | "Train in an environment that is the best you can find." |
| Moses Kiptanui | "If you are not sweating, you are not training." |
| Bro. Colm O'Connell | "Remember, even 13-yr.-old girls are training three times per day." |

| | |
|---|---|
| Simeon Rono | "When you find the weight your body races best at, try and keep it." |
| William Sigei | "Learn to run when feeling the pain; then push harder." |
| Florence Barsosio | "Acclimatize slowly when training in the hot conditions." |
| William Mutwol | "If you run and train as a team, you can defeat anyone." |
| Ibrahim Hussein | "When hill running use your arms and hips to work into a rhythm into the hill." |
| Christopher Kosgei | "Believe you can do it." |
| Paul Tergat | "Ask yourself, 'Can I give more?' The answer is usually 'Yes.'" |
| Peter Rono | "Aim high, and then higher. Training hard—that is all." |

# Economics Of Training

To the Westerner, renting an apartment in Kenya is inexpensive. Exceedingly so, if one wishes to live outside Nairobi or Mombasa. Patrick Rono, a Nandi runner, rents a one-room house in Iten where he lives, often with a fellow runner from his home district. The rent per month, including electricity, is $7. Paul Kanda and Paul Kimutai share a small room and there is another room for their kitchen use, though there is no electricity. They pay a total of $5 per month.

A lot of athletes pay nothing, staying with family members or friends. William Koila, an 800m runner who has had some international success, says, "In the last six months I've had two runners living at my house. The first just turned up, saying he was having difficulties at home and asked if he could stay for a week. I didn't know him, though we'd met briefly at Brother Colm's training camp. That man stayed three months; he never paid for food or rent, nor did he help with any of the jobs."

Not only is the rent cheap but food is too. As noted in the Diet chapter most of what the runners eat is home-grown. When athletes arrive in an area to train they usually bring a sack of produce from their family *shamba*. Lydia Cheromei brought a huge sack of potatoes when she arrived at Brother Colm's.

Even if food has to be paid for, the price is right. In 1996 the cost, in Kenyan shillings, for a two-kilo bag of maize meal was 27 shillings or about 50 U.S. cents. In Europe a one-kilo bag of maize meal would cost the equivalent of 180 Kenyan shillings!

The Kenyan is able, without finance or backing, to give athletics a real shot. The rewards are such that the gamble is well worth it—a season in Europe could result in earnings in excess of ten years' ordinary wages.

More and more assistance is being put forward in Kenya by the athletes who have been successful and earned a good income in the Western world. Three-time Boston Marathon winner Ibrahim Hussein started The Ibrahim Hussein Track Club, a club which provided assistance with training and living expenses to a group of local runners in Nandi District. Frequently the runners would turn up to "borrow" a little money to travel home from the training center. The food was free. Hussein would not reap any financial gain from this venture. "It is our duty to put something back into the sport," he said.

The late 10,000m World Champion Paul Kipkoech had a similar group. "We got transport to any races, or if we needed a ride to a certain hill to do hill training, Paul [Kipkoech] would always provide a vehicle. This was very important because we could not afford to pay for transport. Without Paul we would have never got to any of the races," remembers Joseph Chepkwony, a relative of Olympian Paul Bitok and himself a budding runner. Moses Tanui is another Kenyan distance hero heavily involved in helping the young athletes of the Eldoret area.

Brother Colm O'Connell has virtual "saint" status in Keiyo District. Working half-time at the Teachers Training College in Tamback, Colm spends more than 50% of his wages on his beloved hobby of coaching the junior runners. Driving his car to pick up athletes from group training, following the group in case anyone has to drop out during a training run, transporting runners to races, paying for their food—these and many more expenses are met weekly by Brother Colm without a grumble, and it has been going on for 20 years. There is hardly an athlete in the region who has not been helped by the hand of Brother Colm in some form or another.

# The Training Camp

*There can be few more inspiring training sessions in a runner's life than when charging along the red dirt roads of the Kenyan highlands in glorious sunshine with 50 world-class runners at your side.*

Kenyans generally do not like to live alone. Large families are commonplace in Kenyan rural society. The family base is usually permanent, with the family members building their own houses in close proximity. Because there is an absence of the infrastructure found in many countries in the Western world, Kenyans have learned to rely heavily on family members. Therefore their kindred communal way of life is quite impervious to change.

A Kenyan who is attempting to become an international standard runner will often move to an area with other runners to live and train. Frequently they will travel with another like-minded runner from their village and engage a lodging jointly. Living alone is seen as something incongruous. "I don't like it. All my life I've had lots of people around," says runner Patrick Rono who welcomes Nandi runners to share his single room in Iten.

Residential training camps erupt in the highlands like mushrooms in the dew. "You can not make it to international standard if you are training alone; you need the company of others to push you when you are tired. If you are always training alone your body will take the sessions easier than you should," advised Richard Chelimo who used to train with a large group of Army runners.

All over the Rift Valley Province there are small groups of runners training together. Often an established runner, such as Moses Kiptanui in Nyahururu, bases himself in the area with a couple of training partners. Then others, on hearing that Moses trains there, move to the area. Kenyans still have the hospitable touch, so even the poorest of runners usually manages to find a space to sleep and some *ugali* to eat. "When you run with champions in training, then you know you too can also be a champion," says Ondoro Osoro.

The training camp is thus born. One main advantage of life in a training camp is that the runner is excused from everyday chores. "I moved away from my village to Iten because I could not train with all the jobs at home," tells David Kemei, an international 1500m runner.

Brother Colm adds, "This especially affects women runners in Kenya. Often they run well in school then on returning to the family farm they are faced with all the household work; there is no time or energy left to train." It is not a sight often seen—a woman setting off from the family farm for a training run. "Living in Iten with the Iten running club makes training much easier," notes Lydia Cheromei.

Japhet Kimutai, who has medaled in the World Junior Track & Field Championships, explains, "My parents can not read or understand English; they can not comprehend the chances I have through athletics." Living at home would involve him in work that would preclude effective training; a training camp will help elevate him to world standard.

Kenyans have an amazing ability to relax most of the day; they do not need to be occupied as so many Westerners do. Wilson Musto, one of the Kenyans currently winning many European road races, had a day schedule while training in Sweden which included going back to bed after breakfast and the morning run, rising for lunch before retreating to bed once again, taking an afternoon run, eating dinner, then returning to bed!! Often in the Kenyan countryside children can be seen just sitting by the roadside for great lengths of time doing nothing but watching the world roll by. Therefore at a training camp all energy can be directly channelled into training. Whereas mini-golf or a drive out to some nearby landmark might fill the afternoon of some European athlete away at a training camp, the Kenyan is content to rest up for the next session.

An important role for the camp is for the runners to bond, thus forming a strong team. Before the Armed Forces Championships the coaches sit with the athletes and discuss the use of tactics that will be used during the competition. They draw them up with military precision. Perhaps no other country in the world has athletes who are prepared to give all for their team members in an individual sport such as running. World champion team medalist Simeon Rono tells his own story. "In Durham (1995) I was in great form; I think I could have got a top five individual placing but the orders were that on the third lap I should sprint to the front of the group and push the pace as fast as I could. The end result was that after I had done my effort I faded to 30th place; but anyway we won the team title."

A staggering sacrifice was made by Simon Chemoiywo in the World Cross Country Championships of 1994. "My job was to keep up the pace earlier on, then when Sigei broke from the group not to go after him and take the Ethiopians with me, so I hung back till I was sure Sigei would get to the line before the Ethiopians." Only then did Chemoiywo let loose his lethal kick which left Haile Gebrselassie a well-beaten third. "The important thing for us is that a Kenyan should win; that we must be sure of!" noted Chemoiywo. "When we live, struggle and work together a victory by one of us is for all of us."

The theory is the coaches who have many high-level runners on the team should be able to see which runners best fit their team aspirations at an international championship. Mike Kosgei, who was behind so much of Kenya's success from the mid-80s to the early 90s, had such a close rapport with his athletes that there was almost a family feel to the squad. This was a perfect scenario for getting runners to help each other towards a common goal—team and individual honors. "Kosgei is a master of cross country coaching. He knows it too well that I doubt any other coach can beat him," praises John Ngugi, a man who has a lot to thank Kosgei for.

## The Armed Forces Training Camp

*"Here, the real work is done; Kosgei's three-week camp is just the polish." Coach Albert Masai.*

Thirty kilometers from Nairobi are the N'gong Hills. Resting at high altitude in an environment of lush vegetation sits the Armed Forces training camp. It is here where many large weather-beaten verdant canvas army tents are erected from October through July. The camp is divided into three sections—Army, Navy and Air Force. Each section has its own central office and organization. The three sections train separately and the competition among them is fierce for national Armed Forces track & field and cross country honors. Living full-time at the camp are medical personnel, coaches, athletes and cooks. The cross country and track runners arrive in October; the field athletes in March.

The large tents are basic shelter. There are no ground sheets to keep out the wind and it's not uncommon for the tents to leak. They typically hold 12 to 16 runners. Inside the tents are rows of steel-framed beds. Next to each bed are the athlete's personal belongings locked up in a tin chest. Running apparel is slung over every available space. The conditions are Spartan, or in the words of Paul Tergat, "Here we live like animals."

In the center of each area is the outdoor cooking facility—a large open fire around which the food is prepared each day. The coaches, who are usually superior in military rank to the athletes, live together in one tent. "We are able to understand the athlete much better when we live in constant contact. How else can the coach really get to know his athletes?" questions Navy coach Albert Masai.

The daily routine, Monday through Saturday, goes as follows for the camp's best runners. Others who do not show as much talent or are not producing the best results often have camp chores to take care of, as well as training, such as fetching firewood or sweeping the dirt from the camp.

| | |
|---|---|
| 05:03-06:00 | Rise and run "how you feel." |
| 07:00-07:30 | Stretch and change clothes. |
| 07:45-08:00 | Breakfast. |
| 08:00-09:45 | Relax, usually in bed. |
| 09:45-10:00 | Assemble for training. |
| 10:00-11:15 | Training, the main session. |
| 11:15-11:30 | Stretching/exercises. |
| 11:30-11:50 | Drinking tea, discussing the news of the day. |
| 11:50-13:00 | Relaxing. |
| 13:00-13:30 | Lunchtime. |
| 13:30-15:30 | Relax/sleep, laundry, etc. |
| 15:45-16:45 | Strolling, jogging or exercise. |
| 16:45-17:15 | Showering, cold water basins. |
| 17:15-18:00 | Personal time. |
| 18:00-19:00 | Dinner. |
| 19:00-20:30 | Playing darts, cards or talking. Drink tea or cocoa. |
| 20:30 | Bedtime. |
| 21:00 | Lights out. |

Examples of the main session:

**Winter**. One hour of fartlek, varying efforts from 30 seconds to three minutes • Tempo runs of 50-70 mins at race pace for large portions of the run • Hillwork, intervals or continuous • Steady runs 60-80 mins, though invariably finishing fast • Long run, distance covered would be individual from one hour to three.

**Summer.** 20 x 400m track work at 60-62 sec pace, 45 seconds rest • 3 x 4000m, run at 3-min-per-km speed with a 1-2 min rest • 20 x 800m run at 10km race pace, 1 minute or less rest • A session of 200m intervals, often neither timed or counted • A tempo run of 45 minutes in the forest.

This camp lifestyle has been experienced by the best runners in Kenya. Most of the successful runners, like John Ngugi and Richard Chelimo, have spent time at these camps. Some, such as Paul Tergat, live in close proximity and join the runners just for speed sessions. Others, like Simon Chemoiywo, live and train hundreds of kilometers away, but come into the camp a month before a major competition or simply for sharpening up.

"When you are winning and doing well, the Forces put no demands on you as long as you represent them in the major competitions. There are no military duties for army men such as Ismael Kirui," explains Simeon Rono, one of the team's star cross country runners.

Imagine: on any given day at least 30 world class training partners, food prepared for you daily, live-in coaches and medical staff, high altitude, perfect running climate and an 8-9-month span of living at the training camp each year. Is it any wonder that Kenya is producing such results in the athletics world?

Control over the camp is left to the coaches who often have ranks of senior sergeant or higher. "I don't like loose morals in the camp. Taking one beer or two is okay as long as it does not become a habit, but if there is a lazy runner not committed to hard training then there is no place for him here," says Navy coach Masai.

Certainly a positive atmosphere permeates the camp. Encouragement is showered upon all athletes who are working hard regardless of talent or results, and the harder you train the more respect you gain. The social talk rarely centers on personal achievements but more about life in general, family matters, and plans for the future. Although they have every right to crow a little, Kenyan athletes are very seldom boastful of their running successes.

# The Iten Training Camp

Twice a year, in December and in April, Brother Colm O'Connell, with financial help from Nike, organizes the Iten Training Camp for Kenyan junior runners. The base for the camp is St. Patrick's High School and because the camp is run during the school holidays the setting for a residential camp is perfect. One hundred or so promising juniors are invited to attend the camp which is extremely well organized and successful. A group of coaches are on hand, as is a chaperone for the girls, to supervise the young runners. Brother Colm hires one of the school cooks to remain behind over the holidays to provide three meals a day so the athletes get a chance to train and concentrate fully on running.

Various "celebrity" senior athletes, such as Rose Cheruiyot, Lydia Cheromei and Bernard Barmasai, train with the runners, giving the youngsters a chance to experience the kind of training intensity necessary to reach the top level in the sport. The day is well-planned with activities and guest speakers, such as Moses Kiptanui, Patrick Sang and Christopher Kosgei, who spoke at the December 1995 camp. Many of the athletes benefit from the generous hand of Brother Colm, as they leave the camp with an extra pair of shoes or some athletic clothing.

The majority of the national junior squad for the 1996 World Cross Country Championships came from Brother Colm's camp. "What is positive is that after the first camp, when athletes came from all over Kenya, other camps have sprung up, one in the Kipsigis district, another in Machakos. This is very positive because otherwise the camp would have outgrown itself," says Brother Colm.

The daily schedule runs as follows:

| | |
|---|---|
| 06:00 hrs | Training run. |
| 07:30 hrs | Breakfast, 175 grams of bread and Kenyan tea. |
| 10:00 hrs | Main training session. |
| 11:00 hrs | Morning tea. |
| 11:30 hrs | Talks/lectures. |
| 13:00 hrs | Lunch—vegetables and *ugali*, or rice. |
| 16:00 hrs | Training. |

| 17:00 hrs | Athletics video. |
| 18:45 hrs | Dinner—*ugali*, vegetables and meat. |
| 20:00 hrs | Retire to rooms. |
| 21:00 hrs | Lights out. |

The key words of the camp are discipline, commitment and respect. The athletes are invited to join the camp. There is no payment in monetary terms but the athletes are asked to remember why they are attending the camp. Rules are posted around the school which remind the athletes that they are supposed to attend all the training sessions, fraternize only in their own dormitories, respect the school property, conserve water and keep noise to an acceptable level.

The purpose of the camp is to prepare the runners both physically and mentally for competition, support the young athletes of Kenya, teach training methods to the runners, bring together runners to train as a group, and to have them learn the discipline needed to become a champion runner.

The runners are asked to remember that quality counts over quantity in training and that commitment is expected, so that when they leave the camp they should continue to train. Runners who shows no commitment, or are ill-disciplined may be asked to leave the camp. "Remember, you came to train—athletes keep time," is printed in bold type under the rules.

On the first few days of the camp arriving runners straggle in, all seemingly with complete confidence that they can handle the training and the lifestyle. At bedtime voices and laughter can still be heard. The training sessions are attacked with leonine ferocity. As the days wear on, attendance at the first morning run, as well as the pace, starts to drop; the lights turn off all the quicker in the evening and the runners begin to realize this camp is a challenge, not a holiday. Most runners leave the camp in great shape physically and a better person mentally. Friendships are born and an introduction into the wider world of athletics has been provided.

Brother Colm tries to find one local competition that the runners can attend. At the April camp of 1996 the runners traveled by bus to the Eldoret stadium for a meet. The juniors did exceptionally well. One of Brother Colm's 800m runners, Japhet Kimutai, won the 800m beating both Peter Rono and Nixon Kiprotich—Olympic medalists both!

# The National Training Camp For The World Cross Country Championships

From 1985 to the spring of 1995, Mike Kosgei was the Kenyan national trainer. Kosgei had been a successful athlete himself, and his team thoroughly dominated the World Cross Country Championships. After a second place finish in 1985, the senior men never lost another team title under his reign. Many Kenyans agree that Kosgei's magic was sown, mentally and physically, in the last four weeks before each championship when the training camp was held. All runners selected had to attend. Ismael Kirui, who in 1994 was leading the IAAF World Cross Challenge series, chose to compete instead in Europe and was left off the team despite his status. The camp was run with military discipline by an ex-military man.

High altitude, hills and most importantly, according to Kosgei, suitable dirt roads were the requirements for the proper location in 1994. Embu, on the slopes of Mount Kenya, in the Eastern Province, suited these requirements and it was here, at St. Mark's Teacher Training College, Kosgei would hold his camp. Talking and living daily with his runners Kosgei was able to develop a bond few other national coaches could comprehend. The runners would give everything and more for this man. "The coach must know and feel his runners. He must understand their emotions," explains Kosgei.

The food was similar to the Armed Forces diet—wholesome, plentiful and nourishing. Cooks would be provided to prepare the food but that is where the creature comforts came to an end. The living accommodation was basic school dormitory, metal-framed bed with foam mattress, and a few centrally located taps for water. Washing clothes was also the responsibility of the athlete; this job would usually be done weekly by the male runners, and slightly more often by the females. Attendance at the camp was by invitation only and the costs were covered by the Kenyan Amateur Athletic Association.

*"The mentality is so much different when working with Kenyans. A Kenyan is happy if he or his teammate wins. This makes team tactics much easier than if you are working with a bunch of individuals." Coach Kosgei.*

The hard part of the camp of course was the training. Three sessions per day, six days a week. Sunday was a "rest" day with just one session. The senior men would often log in excess of 240km (140+ miles!) of running in the week. More amazing is the fact that over 30% of that distance would probably be run at a speed comparable to competition pace. Here is the shape of a typical day:

06:00    Morning run. For the men around 10km, for the women 8km, and for a few of the elite, up to 22km. The run would begin at a stumbling pace, though the end of the run was inevitably swift. Kosgei would require the runners to wear short-sleeved t-shirts as preparation for conditions they might have to face at the championships.

07:00    Stretching and exercises, 15-20 mins. A section of the day that Kosgei deemed very important. Flexible bodies lead to more efficient runners, he reasoned. Breakfast then bed.

10:00    Typically the main session. Some examples:

1) 10km fartlek—2 mins fast + 2 mins slow over hilly ground.
2) Road intervals, 100-1000m, no predetermined number. The runners would run till they were "dead."
3) Dirt track intervals, 20 x 400m in 56-64 secs/10 x 800m in 1:58-2:08. Jogging the same distance as recovery.
4) Threshold work, 2 x 5000m at 15 mins pace with 2-3 mins recovery jog.
5) Short intervals, 15km of 3:30 per km warmup(!).
6) Hillwork, 25 x 200m, for senior men, 20 for the women, on a 40-degree hill. Stride back down, no rest!
7) Tempo run, around 20km with an ever-increasing pace. Usually after the first ten minutes it has become a full-blown race situation.
8) 800m repeats. Usually 8-10 repeats run, for the senior men, in about 2 minutes, with an equivalent rest.
9) The long run. Typically between 20-25km. Starting slowly, then the usual creeping up in pace. A hill will often be the starting point for a strong upsurge in pace.

12:00    Lunch, followed by resting. "It is good to lie down; you need rest in hard training," emphasized camp regular Simon Chemoiywo.

16:00    Usually 12-16km of steady running, though often speeding up towards the end. Could also be the main session switched from 10:00 hrs.

18:00   Dinner.
20:30   Bed.

The runners after the interval session, for instance, would include a 5km or so warmdown run. If any of the athletes was not completely exhausted by the earlier session this too would often be run at a high speed.

The camp does have a competitive side. The team would be selected from this group of runners, thus they are of course eager to catch the eye of the coach by "performing" in training. Kenyans can often be quite competitive and it's not uncommon to see a training session turn into a race at any given moment, with or without an audience. "The first time I went to the camp I trained too hard and injured myself; the next time I made sure I did enough to make the team, not more," said Tergat, who admitted to training so hard he thought he was about to faint!

Despite the severe training, recovery seems to be the theme of the camp. The day ends with exhausted bodies strewn about

**Kenyans lead at the 1995 World Championships. Paul Tergat (309) won, Ismael Kirui (305) was 2nd, James Songok (308) was 7th.**

the school, yet mysteriously the next day the legs are again fresh and fit for battle. "This training makes any race seem easy because soon after one session is finished another begins—there is no rest," said Chelimo, perhaps explaining how he managed to "recover" cruising at 62 second laps in 10,000m races!

The month prior to the 1994 World Cross Country Championships is looked at below in day-by-day detail. The morning run, at 6:00 hrs, is excluded due to its individuality. The distances are for the senior men, however some male juniors train just as hard as the seniors. March 1st-26th. Location—St. Mark's College. Mt. Kenya. 6200-ft altitude. Hilly rough terrain. The exercises are done before and after the run. Stretching, in some form, is usually done at least a couple of times a day.

| Date | 10:00 Hrs | 16:00 Hrs |
|---|---|---|
| 01 | 20km @ 80% effort. 20 min rigorous exercises, before and after the run. | 9km fast distance 15 x 200m hill work hard! |
| 02 | 15km "B" speed (75%), finishing fast. | Fartlek 15km, speed "A" (90%+) Stretching, 20 min. |
| 03 | 22km steady +20 mins exercises. | 10km easy + exercises. |
| 04 | 15km high speed. 20 x 100m concentrating on style. | 15km light fartlek + exercises. |
| 05 | 15km high speed + 20 strength exercises. | 8km easy. |
| 06 | Competition, cross country 13km. | Rest. |
| 07 | 12km 75% effort, finishing fast +20 min exercises. | Strolling. |
| 08 | 12km easy + circuit training. | 20km @ 6 min/ mile + 20 min exercises. |
| 09 | 12km high speed fartlek + 20 min stretch. | 12km warm-up, 30 x 150m hill work + exercises. |
| 10 | 25km hilly distance run, "supposed" to be relatively easy. | Strolling, washing clothes, etc. |
| 11 | 18km high speed, 90% effort, racing tempo. | 12km fartlek @ 75% effort. |
| 12 | 15km @ 80% effort + 20 min exercises. | 12km competition speed, flat-out. |
| 13 | 20km high speed. | Strolling/jogging. |
| 14 | 15km run in around 50 min, hilly + hard. | As above. |
| 15 | 10km easy. | 10km easy. |
| 16 | 15km fast + 15 x 100m @ 85% effort. | 10km fartlek, 80% . effort + exercises. |

| | | |
|---|---|---|
| 17 | 10km steady + 20 min strength exercises. | 8km jog + 20 min exercises. |
| 18 | 18km long run, again hypothetically run at a "conversational" pace. | 8km easy jog. |
| 19 | 10km @ 80% effort. | 10km easy + exercises. |
| 20 | 10km fartlek + exercises. | 8km easy + exercises. |
| 21 | 15km @ 80-85% effort + exercises. | 10km @ 80% + exercises. |
| 22 | 15km high speed, tough and hard. | 10km @ 80% effort. |
| 23 | TRAVEL. | |
| 24 | TRAVEL. | 8km easy jog. |
| 25 | 10km jog on the course "looking and learning." Running together. | Strolling. |
| 26 | Morning jog as a team. | World Championship domination. |

The Kenyans are well aware of their reputation and the respect that accompanies them, A canny pre-race tactic is the group jog. Like a pride of lions they prowl the course reminding the opposition of their united force. A similar "tactic" is employed prior to the national championships. As the senior men await the start, the Armed Forces runners jog to the line with a flag bearer leading them as they chant in unison to remind their opposition— "Together we shall win."

True to their word, win they do!

# The Barcelona Steeplechase Training Camp

The runners selected for the 1992 Olympic steeplechase event for the Kenyan team were Matthew Birir, Patrick Sang and William Mutwol. As two of the three were not affiliated with the Armed Forces, the three decided to train together independent of the Forces. The three lived sharing a single room. Sleeping, eating and training together, a powerful bond was woven between the men prior to the games. "If we ran intervals we would run multiples of three so we would all take equal efforts," remembered Sang.

Moving to Spain the runners again shared a room. The race and the result was a team effort: gold, silver and bronze. Mutwol, as planned, drew out a fast pace; Sang and Birir pushed on in the latter part making sure William was tucked in behind them. More often than not when Europeans train together, the training becomes too competitive—more like a psych-out. Here is the difference with the Kenyans. "My bronze was Birir's bronze," explained Mutwol.

Would the Kenyans dominate without training camps? Due to the Kenyan mentality of training and living together, the runners would succeed in any case, as lots of small "camps" would be formed. Certainly, however, larger camps do help create dominance in numbers. "When you are tired there is always another man pushing and not letting you rest. Even if you think you are at full speed you can always be pushed a little faster, " said Daniel Komen.

**Coaches Mike Kosgei and Brother Colm O'Connell at St. Patrick's school. Photo by the author.**

# The Kenyan Diet

Sunshine bathes the Kenyan fields, and purifying rainfall nourishes the land. The chemicals that saturate fields in the so-called developed quarters of the world are less common here. Farmers have financial difficulty enough trying to hire a tractor for plowing, let alone investing in quantities of expensive chemicals. The climate is advantageous for growing hearty crops. Maize grown in Kenya larger than corn grown, say, in England and looks far more edible, flushed by the sun rather than by alkaline.

The price of land in Kenya is much more affordable than, for instance, a car. Most rural Kenyans own a plot of land called a *shamba*. This enables the family to produce their own food. 1996 Army brigades steeplechase champion William Kiprono explains, "We grow enough maize to eat the year round; it is sufficient just for home use. Like our neighbors we don't grow to sell." When Rose Cheruiyot first began to make money from running one of the first things she did was to buy 25 acres for a family *shamba*. Kenyans often prefer to invest in the land rather than in the bank. "Inflation and economics are not so stable in Kenya," explains Paul Tergat.

The diet common to the average family from the rural towns and villages, where virtually all Kenyan runners grow up and live, is quite nutritious. But this is often because of economics, not necessarily by preference. "I love french fries, I don't like *ugali* at all," admits Lydia Cheromei. "Hamburgers are great; I like to eat at the fast food places when I'm living in London," smiles Benson Koech. "My favorite? A big steak with a plate of chips (french fries)," says Kip Cheruiyot. Kimutai Koskei, a 28:49 10,000m runner, gained over 10kgs when posted to Bosnia for six months. "We had fried food everyday and I grew to love it!"

The depth of the pocket is usually the dictator in Kenya. There are well-documented cases of some Kenyan athletes becoming chronic alcoholics after earning vast sums of money, and in some cases it is the same with food. Often the richer the athlete the more varied his plate. With the current generation of runners nearly all coming from poor origins, this ensures at least 20 years of good food into their bodies.

# Key Diet Ingredients Of A Typical Rift Valley Resident

Maize is the main crop of the Kenyan farmer. It requires little attention and thrives in the Kenyan climate. Once harvested, the maize is removed from the cob, dried for a number of months, then ground to form a flour called maize meal flour which is cooked to produce the staple food of kenya—*ugali*. From the *shamba* the maize meal is unsifted and rough in texture, but when bought commercially it is usually sifted and of a fine consistency. Some cobs are saved for roasting over an open fire to be eaten as a lunch, and some maize is boiled with kidney beans to be eaten as *githeri*, a lunch dish.

| | |
|---|---|
| Ugali | A stiff porridge made from water and ground maize. Eaten at least once a day. Used as a Westerner would rice or pasta. |
| Sukuma Wiki | Dark green cabbage plant. Eaten with *ugali*. Often mixed with wild dark green plants that grow on the *shamba*. |
| Uji | Porridge made from ground maize or millet, often fermented. |
| Maziwa Lala | Fermented fresh milk. |
| Viasi | Potatoes, often sweet potatoes, at lunchtime. |
| Maharagwe | Kidney beans, frequently eaten for lunch. |
| Githeri | Maize and kidney beans mixed and boiled together. |
| Muthokoi | Similar to *githeri* but with pumpkin leaves and potatoes added. |
| Machungwa | Oranges, regularly eaten when green in color. |
| Chai | Tea, the leaves boiled with milk and sugar. |

The nutritional value of the above foods provides an adequate diet, excellent for the runner. The *ugali* is pure carbohydrate. *Mboga*, (green vegetables such as *sukuma wiki*), provide a plentiful source of iron and minerals. Proteins are found in abundance in the *maziwa lala* and *maharagwe*. Vitamins come from the vegetables and the *machungwa*. The fat content is extremely low. When boiling the *maziwa* (milk), the fat is skimmed from the surface and used for cooking.

# Pills And Supplements

Increasingly, athletes from all corners of the globe are taking substances to enhance performance. Athletic journals are often advertising some new potion that is certain to improve performance. Not so in Africa! Firstly the information is very sparse in Kenya. There are no running magazines available and the information on the most fundamental of matters is hard to come by. Apart from basic glucose powder, which Sally Barsosio admits was an inspiration to keep on competing (as the sweet powder was often served at the end of a race), substances, such as creatine or Q10, are simply not sold.

Vitamins and/or minerals are taken by a few of the runners who have lived abroad for a length of time, but even these are rare cases. Over in Europe where a manager may pressure one of his runners to take supplements, a Kenyan's easy-going nature probably would make him acquiesce. But in Kenya, the tablets would undoubtedly be left untaken. Most Kenyans know that the real secret to success is hard training. "There is no substitute to hard training, and more hard training," said Moses Kiptanui. Asked whether he used any sports drink while running and winning the 1996 Boston Marathon, Moses Tanui replied, "Just plain water!"

The Kenyans have a drug far more powerful—that of belief. It is not ignorance, far from it. It is the key factor in their bodily maintenance. They feel that with their training and way of life they can be unbeatable. "Look at the European athletic results; should we start doing what they are doing to "improve" our results?" chuckles Army coach Kiplimo who has studied biology in England.

There have been, in Kenya's athletic history, just a couple of drug infringement incidents. These cases in Kenya have been ordinarily for a drug found in Kenyan common cold solutions available at most apothecaries around the country. "It is one thing we stress very carefully at our training camps; there isn't the information available when you go to the chemist [pharmacist] on what substances are banned and what aren't," says Brother Colm. Even the hospital in Iten, in one of Kenya's major running centers, was unable to come up with a list of banned substances. Therefore it is highly conceivable that a Kenyan can be an accidental victim, since strict testing is enforced by the IAAF in Kenya the year round. Japhet Kimutai, a 17-year old schoolboy, barely managed to find a race in Europe in the 1996 season, but he was hunted down in the Kenyan highlands during the spring of 1996 by the drug testers. A member of the drug testing group, who wished to remain anonymous says, "Because of their incredible achievements we are pressured by other countries' athletic bodies to test, and re-test, the Kenyan athletes to 'find' some excuse for their achievements. They are tested more often than most other athletes and 99.9% come up clean!"

# *Typical Daily Diets*

While the Western world moves away from the idea of eating excesses of red meat, cooking oil, fats and salt, the Kenyans have no such notions. The Armed Forces training camps chefs are heavy-handed with the fats, salts and oils. The beef stew is dripping in oil, red meat is served twice a day well salted, and the morning sandwiches have a slab of margarine plastered on them. Western nutritionists would be diving for their stomach pumps after day on the camp!

If a family has money to spare, bread will be eaten for breakfast, though this is a luxury, and one most families go without. "We sometimes have bread at Christmas and on New Year's Day," says marathoner Mark Yatich. Most families buy just tea and sugar from the shop and grow their other supplies. Meat is another luxury commodity; most families are lucky to eat meat once or twice a month. The usual meat is *kondoo* (sheep), though at ceremonies *ngombe* (cow), would be eaten. "It used to be that if a visitor came, an animal from the farm was slaughtered; however poverty does not allow that. We had only five cows and a couple of chickens, so we ate meat only a couple of times per year, though because we were typical of the neighborhood we did not miss it," remembers Julius Korir.

Three examples of daily diets are given below. Diet #1 is taken from an athlete named Paul Kanda. Kanda has no income, has a small piece of shared land on which to grow maize, and relies on friends and family for any extra money needed. Kanda is typical of many Kenyan athletes who are trying to reach international standard. Diet #2 is taken from a day in the life of Moses Tanui. Tanui is a well-to-do successful runner. Diet #3 is a day's menu for the Armed Forces training camp. Many of Kenya's best runners, for instance Moses Kiptanui, Moses Tanui, William Tanui, Paul Tergat, Paul Bitok, Ismael Kirui and Richard Chelimo, have developed at the camp—so it must be a recipe for attainment!

## DIET#1

| | | |
|---|---|---|
| Breakfast | 8:00 hrs | Two cups of black sugared tea. |
| Mid-morning* | 11:00 hrs | One cup of *uji* |
| Lunch | 13:00 hrs | *Ugali* and *sukuma wiki* |
| Dinner | 19:00 hrs | *Ugali* and *sukuma wiki* |

* This would only be taken if Kanda was training three times a day as was his usual practice. Occasionally a neighbor or friend would donate a piece of meat or a jug of milk. However these occurrences were neither regular or plentiful.

## DIET #2

| | | |
|---|---|---|
| Breakfast | 7:00 hrs | Bread, jam and margarine sandwiches. Kenyan tea. |
| Mid-morning | 11:00 hrs | Kenyan tea |
| Lunch | 13:00 hrs | Rice, bananas and a beef vegetable stew, followed by more Kenyan tea. |
| Dinner | 19:00 hrs | *Ugali* with meat and vegetables. |

## DIET #3

| | | |
|---|---|---|
| Breakfast | 7:00 hrs | White bread and margarine, lots of Kenyan tea. |
| Mid-morning | 11:00 hrs | At least a couple of mugs of Kenyan tea. |
| Lunch | 13:00 hrs | A blend of rice, potatoes and spaghetti with kidney beans and chunks of beef in an oily sauce. Kenyan tea. |
| Dinner | 19:00 hrs | A large slab of *ugali*, potatoes and a beef stew. Kenyan tea or cocoa. |

The amounts eaten are frequently substantial. Kenyans do not typically worry about weight control; they believe hard training will take care of that. The regular-sized plate at the camp is usually heaped with food. The Kenyan women are a little more concerned about overeating than the men. Lydia Cheromei believes that during the cross country season her weight is not really a concern, though for the track season she makes an effort to reduce weight. "You need more strength to get up the hills and through the mud, but on the track it is important to be light." A week before finishing second in the World Cross Country Championships Rose Cheruiyot was attempting to slim down a couple of kilos, one day substituting a lemon for lunch.

## *Diet On The Road*

World Cross Country Championship silver medalist Simon Chemoiywo spends a large part of the summer months in Europe. Based in the London suburb of Teddington, Simon has adapted, along with a houseful of Kenyans, to British life. When asked about the differences in diet, Chemoiywo pointed out that the basic structure, and most of the food types, were similar to what he would eat at home on his farm near Kipkabus. "We shop at the local supermarket. The big difference is all the selections of brands for each article. We usually buy bags of rice, potatoes, corn meal flour to make *ugali*, vegetables, bread and meat." Sometimes if the runners are out for a stroll or away from home, then they eat out for lunch, though most of them try to make it back to the base for the important evening meal.

"We can go to one of the fast food restaurants and take a hamburger and chips. They taste very good and it is a light meal," says Lydia Cheromei, one of the many Kenyans who very much enjoy Western fast food. A sample of a typical Teddington day for Chemoiywo would be:

| | |
|---|---|
| Breakfast | A couple of slices of toast with margarine. Tea. |
| Mid-morning | Tea. |
| Lunch | Vegetable soup. |
| Dinner | Vegetables and meat, with either *ugali*, rice or potatoes. |

Simeon Rono, another London-based Kenyan from the national cross country squad, adds, "When we are racing on the track we usually do not eat as much as when we are in heavy training. I have to watch that I don't go up in weight with the reduced training. But when we are a big group it helps as we are all watching each other. If I am 65kgs then I know I will not run good, but if I am 62 . . . aah! We all know at what weight we perform our best at and we try to keep that weight constant. There have been many cases of our countrymen coming over and eating their way out of form. They arrive at a hotel where for breakfast you can eat as much as you want. Maybe all their lives food has been scarce; the temptation can be big."

Some of the runners are a little superstitious about the power of *ugali*. Some even go as far as believing that Kenyan *ugali* is more powerful than European versions. The night before an important race a bag of maize meal flour brought over from Kenya is often opened on Back Road in Teddington as the runners gather round the "magic" food. Jane Kimutai, a 400m runner who in 1995 was voted the Kenyan schools' most valuable athlete, is one such superstitious athlete. Jane even goes as far as saying that if salt is taken with the *ugali* then the runner will not be able to run. One can salt the accompanying vegetables, however, with impunity!

# A Blood Link!

Ingrid Kristiansen was a fond eater of blood pudding. Nutritionists have often wondered about the benefits of eating such foods with a high blood content. Then came the news that the Chinese world record breaking women drank turtle blood daily to strengthen their bodies against the hard training. The Kenyans are at it too! The Maasai tribe, who are spread over the Southern Rift Valley, have long been known to drink cow's blood mixed with milk. The fresh milk, from the cow, is blended with blood taken from the throat of a living beast with a thin pipe, mixed and drunk. Blood is also drunk straight.

The Air Force camp was expecting some superior to visit their training center. It was decided to slaughter a goat in their honor and cook up a stew. The goat was hung up on a nearby tree and manually gutted. As the fresh warm blood flowed from the animal, a soldier collected the liquid in a large cup. A group of runners (not just the Maasai) gathered round and each took a gulp of blood before passing the cup along.

Kenyans do not particularly like sweet foods. Chocolates are often accepted with great relish then surreptitiously spit out. Confectioneries are not common in the diet of young Kenyans as they are for so many Western children, thus many Kenyans never develop a palate for such foods. An Army 10,000m runner named Kosgei remembers his first, and last, encounter with chocolate. "I won a box of chocolates in a race in Finland, so in the evening when I was back at my hotel room I opened the box and ate them. The next day I was feeling very bad in the stomach. If I were to take this food to my children and friends and they were to experience such feelings they would think me a bad man for giving them such food, so I threw the rest of the box away."

# Kenyan Running Success—
# Some Roots And Reasons

## Tribal Affiliations

Kenya is made up of many different ethnic groups, ranging from huge tribes with millions of members, like the Kikuyu, to small ones with only a little more than a thousand members. Most of Kenya's runners come from the tribes listed below. [N.B. Many thanks to John Manners for enhancements and amendments to the lists below.]

- **KALENJIN**  Homeland in Western Rift Valley Province; population about 3 million, 10-11% of the national total, fourth or fifth largest tribe. Runners are listed according to their sub-tribe.

**Nandi**  Kip Keino, Henry Rono, Wilson Kipketer, Mike Boit, Moses Tanui, Paul Kipkoech, Ibrahim Hussein, Patrick Sang, Sammy Lelei, Julius Korir, Paul Bitok, Kimeli Kipkemboi, Joseph Tengelei, Peter Koech, Peter Rono, Philip Barkutwo, David Kibet, Paul Ruto, Joshua Kipkemboi, Gideon Chirchir, Joseph Keter, Eliud Barngetuny, Ezekiel Bitok, Pamela Chepchumba.

**Marakwet**  Moses Kiptanui, Ismael Kirui, Richard Chelimo, William Mutwol, Catherine Kirui, Joseph Kibor.

**Tugen**  Matthew and Jonah Birir, Paul Tergat, Charles and Kip Cheruiyot, Nixon Kiprotich, Lydia Cheromei.

**Kipsigis**  Robert Kibet, Helen Chepngeno, William Sigei, Sammy Langat, Charles Tangus, William Kalya, Simeon Rono, Dominic Kirui, Wilson Kiprugut.

**Keiyo**  Simon Chemoiywo, Rose Cheruiyot, Daniel Komen, Sally and Florence Barsosio, Joseph

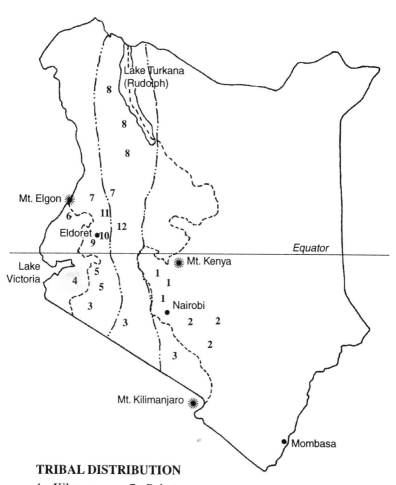

- - - - - - - Rift Valley Provincial Boundary

—··—··— Rim of Geological Rift Valley

Lake Turkana
(Rudolph)

8

8

8

Mt. Elgon  7  7

6  11

Eldoret  12

9  10

Lake Victoria  4

5

5

3

3

3

Mt. Kenya

Equator

1

1

1

Nairobi

2  2

2

Mt. Kilimanjaro

Mombasa

**TRIBAL DISTRIBUTION**

| 1 | Kikuyu | 7 | Pokot |
|---|--------|---|-------|
| 2 | Kamba | 8 | Turkana |
| 3 | Maasai | 9 | Nandi |
| 4 | Gusii (Kisii) | 10 | Keiyo |
| 5 | Kipsigis | 11 | Marakwet |
| 6 | Sabaot | 12 | Tugen |

|        |                                                              |
|--------|--------------------------------------------------------------|
|        | Chesire, Susan Sirma, Christopher Kosgei, Benson Koech.      |
| **Sabaot** | Shem Kororia, Kipyego Kororia, Ben Jipcho, Samson Kimobwa, Andrew Masai. |
| **Pokot**  | Tegla Loroupe, Wilson Musto, Simon Lopuyet. |

- **GUSII or KISII**  Homeland in Nyanza Province, west of Rift Valley Province. Population about 1.6 million, 5 or 6% of national total, sixth largest tribe. Delilah Asiago, Josephat Machuka, Yobes Ondieki, Naftali Temu, Ondoro Osoro, Thomas Osano, Philip Mosima, Zakaria Nyambaso, Wilfred Kirochi, Julius Ondieki, Lameck Aguta.

- **KAMBA**  Homeland in Eastern Province, just east of Nairobi. Population about 3 million, 10-11% of national total. Fourth or fifth largest tribe. Cosmas and Josephat Ndeti, William Musyoki, Benson Masya, Jimmy Muindi, Joseph Nzau, Mike Musyoki.

- **KIKUYU**  Homeland in Central Province, north of Nairobi. Population about 6.3 million, about 21% of national total. Kenya's largest tribe. John Ngugi, Douglas Wakiihuri, Laban Chege, Joseph Kamau, Julius Kariuki, Ibrahim Kinuthia, Gladys Wamuyu, Joseph Kimani, James Kariuki.

- **MAASAI**  Homeland in Southern Rift Valley Province. Population about half a million, 1.5-2% of national total. Ninth largest tribe. Billy and Patrick Konchellah, Stephen Ole Marai.

- **TURKANA**  Homeland in Northern Rift Valley Province. Population about 400,000, 1-1.5% of national total. Tenth largest tribe. Paul Ereng.

Most years about three-fourths of the members of the national cross country team come from the Rift Valley Province. In 1996 the winning junior women's team came from just one district in the province: Keiyo District. This is without doubt due to the enormous amount of work Brother Colm has put into the district and nearby parts of the province.

# Altitude

A lot has been written about the effects of training at altitude. Scientists generally agree that being born and living at altitude provide some advantage to the long distance runner. Exactly how much help is impossible to quantify, but it's worth noting that much of Western Kenya is at significant altitude, and this is certainly true of all the training bases used by Kenyan elite runners.

| CITY/TOWN | ALTITUDE | ATHLETES TRAINING |
|-----------|----------|-------------------|
| Eldoret | 2100m | Moses Tanui |
| Eldama Ravine | 2100m | Lydia Cheromei |
| Iten | 2300m | Benson Koech |
| Kamariny | 2400m | William Mutwol |
| Kapsabet | 1950m | Ibrahim Hussein |
| Kaptagat | 2400m | Fila Team |
| Machakos | 1600m | Cosmas Ndeti |
| Nandi Hills | 2000m | Peter Rono |
| N'gong Hills | 2000m | Paul Tergat |
| Nyahururu | 2350m | Moses Kiptanui |
| Kipkabus | 2200m | Simon Chemoiywo |

Machakos, lowest on the list, is surrounded by the Mua Hills. When training, therefore, Ndeti is often well above the 2000m level.

Says Brother Colm O'Connell, who coaches in the highland village of Iten, "There are a number of factors which make the Kenyans the runners they are. Altitude and the good climate do play an important role."

# The Weather

The lowlands, such as the coastal region, have produced no high-caliber distance runners. The climate of such places is highly unfavorable to long distance running. The climate of the highlands is conducive to training almost year-round. Although the sun is hot, a low humidity makes running pleasantly comfortable. During the rainy period, June to August, the mud roads can be challenging to run on as they become like a sticky dough—though the Kenyans believe that this helps to build leg strength.

By mid-morning the powerful sun has usually dried the roads again for the runner wishing to avoid such surfaces.

At high altitudes the nights and early mornings can be chilly. Some coaches use the shivery 6:00am sessions to acclimatize runners to the weather to be expected in European cross country races. At a training camp held at St. Patrick's during a school holiday, all runners had to run in shorts and just a t-shirt in the cold. For this reason Benson Koech lists Iten as his favorite training residence. "The weather here is similar to the European summer, so we can go across with the least of climatic changes."

The quality sessions are reserved for the warmth of mid-morning; the sun is already high in the sky and it can be scorching, but with low humidity. This is the time for the hard workout.

With the warm climate hard training is easier to accomplish, as Kenyans who have tried to survive over a Northern European winter have often learned to their peril. Cosmas Ndeti lost a valuable week's training in his 1996 build up to the Boston Marathon when he traveled to train with his friend Benson Masya in England. Heavy snow meant quality training was impossible. Meanwhile back in Kenya blue skies and a warm sun make those long runs much more endurable. Of course the weather can get too hot, but at least the athlete has the option of running in the mid-morning and late afternoon, thus avoiding the hottest noontime sun.

The Kenyans do not like to run in the rain. There is a belief that the water will get into the chest causing a cold. "It is better to miss one training session than a whole week through catching flu," explained Nicholas Twolongut, an Air Force marathoner. "We sleep in if we hear the rain," relates Kirwa Tanui, explaining why the camp was without movement one rainy morning. The previous day over 80 runners sat in their tents waiting to see if the weather would clear up sufficiently for their mid-morning training run. Usually it does, since the rain in Kenya falls more often than not in the afternoon. The athletes who live over the summer in London, for example, have to adapt to training in the rain. On returning to Kenya they soon revert to the Kenyan ways.

# A Walking Heritage

The heritage of most tribes in Rift Valley Province is pastoral, with the common activity working with large herds of livestock. The stock must often be moved to new grazing grounds, since water can be scarce and often great distances must be covered to seek it. From a young age children are saddled with that responsibility and can find themselves as youngsters walking vast distances. Nicholas Twolongut remembers his childhood. "I had to take the sheep to the market. The walk would take all morning. I would begin at daylight and reach the market near midday. On the days when there was no market I was walking with the goats. If I didn't do these jobs, I would be beaten by my father. These tasks began when I was six years old."

Traveling in Kenya is usually on foot, unless of course one is going great distances. Kenyans' notions of "a walking distance" are rather farther than the average Westerner's. Three or four hours of walking to visit a friend for a cup of tea and a chat are not events that raise an eyebrow. Roads for vehicular traffic in many cases do not even lead to the village.

The speed of the journey is dictated by the urgency of the destination. "I ran to school to avoid a caning for being late," says Lydia Cheromei. If she was early leaving the house then she would walk to school, but more often than not, for which today she is thankful, she was late and ran most of the way. "I never ran to school; I lived only 400m away," says one of Kenya's most successful female runners, Rose Cheruiyot, dispelling the myth that all Kenyan runners travel, if not run, great distances to school! Some run to school because they enjoy running but the percentage is low. It's undeniable, however, that early dependence on shank's mare makes a great foundation for an endurance-based sporting future.

## Tradition And Belief

Tribal tradition also makes a difference. Kenyans believe they are capable of what their tribesmen have been capable of. Hilary Choge, captain of the University of Nairobi athletic team, spoke of his belief. "I had tried many sports but I always knew that if I wanted to be a runner I could be, simply because I was a Nandi and we have had so many great runners from our district." There are next to no runners from the Luo tribe who live near Lake Victoria to the west of the Rift Valley. The Luos believe themselves to be great footballers. Always there is an exception to the rule, of course. Jackton Odhiambo Wasiema is an up and coming Luo runner. Odhiambo, however, is a longtime resident of Eldoret—not of the Luo homeland.

# Attitude Not Altitude

Coach Mike Kosgei believes that there has been too much emphasis by Western observers on altitude and not enough on the staggering work load the Kenyans regularly undertake. "People think you just have to be born a Kenyan to be a champion runner!" laughs Kosgei. "If it were altitude alone then why are there not a lot of great runners from Nepal or Peru?"

Certainly the proof of the pudding can be seen when one compares the runners of Tanzania and Uganda to Kenya. Although both countries are adjacent to Kenya and have high altitude regions, the differences in athletic ability are extreme. Uganda has just a few athletes competing, and Tanzania has a similar standard of distance success to many European countries, but nothing like Kenya's success. In the World Cross Country team championships of the last ten years the Tanzanian senior men have never been medalists whereas the Kenyans have taken gold every year! Of course Kenya has long had a stable government, organized training camps, hard-working athletes, and a pervasive tradition of endurance running. Tanzania has had world-ranked runners in the past and with the same "advantages" could perhaps rival the Kenyans. Altitude is not the only factor.

Being from Kenya also furnishes a psychological edge. Athletes have been known to freeze upon hearing that a "dreaded" Kenyan is in the race. John Lory Masongo, a Tanzanian champion over the half-marathon distance with a best time of 61:18, told how he and his teammates tried to avoid races against their "neighbors." "One time I ran in the Kenyan national cross country championships. . . Ooh, I was a long way behind. Never again!" That year Lory was undefeated in Tanzania.

While it stands to reason that the altitude-accommodated body of the East African highlander plays some part in Kenya's running success, the answer to the question about favorable environment and climate must be that they are instrumental but not exclusive players. As has been said by Kosgei, "It is attitude, not altitude."

# Born To Run?

A film crew arrived in Eldoret prior to the 1996 Olympics, there to film a documentary about Kenyan runners. The director wanted a few changes. "Can you please remove your track suits and run with bare legs?" came the request. "Can we have some cows roaming free on the field where the runners are training?" "Can you sing while you run in the group?" And finally, "Can you remove your shoes and run barefoot?"

In my previous month of training with this group of students, there had been no bare legs on training runs, no cows mingling with runners, absolutely no singing (or talking) during running and not a single barefoot runner! This "documentary" film wouldn't be interesting enough, in the mind of the director, if it didn't conform to his preconceived notions.

Westerners have many preconceived ideas as to the whys and wherefores of Kenyan running success. Here are some of them:

- It's the living and training at high altitude.
- Kenyans have a toughness born of early hardship and/or they have been endurance-trained from an early age because of running to/from school, tending the flocks, running from lions.
- There has to be some genetic or physiological advantage. Otherwise, why doesn't the hard training lead to injury and breakdown?
- Kenyans have a long tradition in distance running, with few other  sports to lose potential runners to. Kenyan youngsters take to running the way American kids play basketball or baseball.

The truth is there is no one factor that anyone can say is responsible for Kenyan running success; it's a combination of factors, including intense training, altitude and climate, rugged upbringing, and tradition, plus a nutritious diet, the training camps, the monetary incentives on the international circuit, the competitive nature of the Nandi and of the Kalenjin in general, and a longtime political stability in the country (along with government support of the sport).

A genetic or physiological factor has not been isolated to anyone's satisfaction. Indeed, the Kenyan coaches would tell you that Kenyan runners do not get injured as much as Westerners because so much of their training is done on those forgiving dirt roads and paths.

For every Kenyan runner who succeeds, there are dozens who fail, as it is everywhere. It's a minority who make the national level. The Rift Valley AAA held a track meet in Eldoret when I was there. The Kenyan event, the steeplechase, had over 25 entrants. Fewer than 10 made it to the finish!

Though there are a large number of runners in proportion to the total population, public interest in the sport is well behind soccer football and even cricket. When the Kenyan cross country team won the World Championship in South Africa, the results were not broadcast on the evening radio sports roundup program. You had to wait until the following day to get the result. On the other hand, the African Football Championships, without a Kenyan team participating, were shown live on TV every day of the tournament.

Paul Tergat says, "You will see why we win if you train with us." Kenyans work harder and have the inspiration of Kenyan middle and long distance records being broken year in year out. All similar British records were set in the 1980s, only two German records were established in the 90s (both by Dieter Baumann)

### Comparison of Men's National Records (Years Set), as of 12/31/96

| Event | Britain | Kenya | Germany | USA |
|---|---|---|---|---|
| 800m | 1981 | 1996* | 1983 | 1985 |
| 1000m | 1981 | 1995 | 1980 | 1974 |
| 1500m | 1985 | 1996 | 1980 | 1985 |
| 1 mile | 1985 | 1992 | 1988 | 1982 |
| 2000m | 1985 | 1992 | 1982 | 1987 |
| 3000m | 1982 | 1996 | 1995 | 1996 |
| 3000m St | 1988 | 1995 | 1987 | 1985 |
| 5000m | 1982 | 1996 | 1995 | 1996 |
| 10,000m | 1988 | 1994 | 1983 | 1986 |
| Marathon | 1985 | 1995 | 1988 | 1981 |

*Wilson Kipketer, now a Danish citizen, established this record while still a Kenyan.

and two American records in the 90s (both by Bob Kennedy). The longest-standing Kenyan distance record dates to 1992!

If there is any one factor to emphasize it is hard training, followed by hard training. Kenyans set no limits. A single week may involve seven straight days of hard workouts. "Rest when the body is tired and worn down, not when your body is strong and can take more training," reasoned Christopher Kosgei. And Julius Korir adds, "I trained hard, hard, hard before I could run well at all; people think we were born running but it is not true."

If you insist on having a Kenyan "training secret," try this one as the reason Kenyans seem to have such a high pain threshold. A large percentage of the Kalenjin runners are circumcised by traditional methods, i.e., without anaesthetic and with no crying. The 13-15-year old sits in silence while the elders perform the ceremony. "Whenever I think I am in pain during running, I remember the pain of my circumcision," says a Kipsigis runner. "The pain when running does not compare. Kenyans have no pain barrier after circumcision. My father told me to remember the pain and gain knowledge that I could face any pain with my eyes open after that ceremony!"

Now, Western runners, there's a Kenyan "training secret" for you to copy!

# A Day At The Races

"All Kenyans want to run their best in the nationals. Not only is it the golden ticket to exposure, but for most of us it is our family's only chance to see us compete." Paul Tergat.

"The nationals are like nothing else. You have over 200 of the best Kenyans fighting like crazy, like a cavalry charge." Patrick Sang.

"Today I run for the Armed Forces team. Of course, we will win; sure—we always do!" Ismael Kirui.

"It pains me to be here watching. Last year I was number three. I have slept for four straight days with illness—totally out, otherwise I would be running." Simon Chemoiywo.

"Man, incredible running here today, amazing stuff." Double World Cross Country Champion John Treacy of Ireland.

It is the day prior to the Kenyan 1996 National Cross Country Championships, an event which is the most competitive cross country race in the world. Very few foreigners bother to enter this competition; the ones who do never feature at the sharp end of the field. The setting for the championships is N'gong Race Track, usually reserved for race horses. It is some 20 kilometers upland from the bustling capital city, Nairobi. At an altitude of 1800m the air is thin but fresh.

Ten kilometers farther up the road, away from Nairobi, are the N'gong Hills. . . and the Armed Forces training camp. The mood at the camp is subdued the morning before the day of the championships. The runners have either taken an early morning jog or are resting completely as tomorrow brings the most significant competition of the cross country season. Over the last three months the hours sweated and heaped upon many other hours have left sore muscles and memories of painful effort.

The talk centers upon race tactics. The Armed Forces will enter a number of teams. Their elite squad is highly favored to win the title. Challenging will be runners from the Rift Valley Province team and those from the prisons and the police, who always put up strong teams. The Armed Forces coaches had lived, slept and eaten this competition throughout the last few months, preparing and nurturing the runners. The pressure is on.

"If the team loses the coaches will be blamed; their job is to win this competition. A lot of high ranking military officials will be at the race tomorrow so it is a good time to try and pick up a promotion!" reveals Simeon Rono of the national squad.

An Australian television crew here in Kenya to film a documentary are stopped on the road leading to the camp. Since the camp first and foremost is a military base, cameras and foreigners are not always welcome. The crew decides to film by the roadside, and a handful of athletes oblige the lenses by dressing in tracksuits, showing off with some jogging strides.

A new white Subaru slips along the road and pulls into camp. Clothed in casual slacks and a cotton print shirt, Paul Tergat, the 1995 World Champion, alights with a relaxed smile. Munching on a mango, Paul speaks about the nationals. "It is important for me to be seen to run the nationals tomorrow. Of course, the main race for myself is in three weeks in South Africa. The training has been going well; I am not training as hard as I have been in the past but I feel the form is very good. Tomorrow we will see." It is obvious by Tergat's body language and facial expressions that nerves will not be a factor for the defending champion. The confidence comes from an excellent winter's training.

Tergat's visit was primarily to pick up his competition number along with the white, red and blue team kit. He leaves soon afterward to spend the afternoon relaxing at home with his family, a kilometer down the road.

The runners mention other individuals who may reach the podium. Josephat Machuka is a name often heard. Machuka comes from Kisii District and runs for the Sportsmark Club. "Machuka can be brilliant or bad; he will try to win the race with front running; he is one of few who has the talent to do it, but I don't think so!" predicts Joseph Kibor. Kibor is a leading figure on the Armed Forces main team. He has run well in their selection race and earlier in the Armed Forces Championships. He is perhaps best known for selling his goat to earn the fare to the Commonwealth Games trials in 1990.

The subdued atmosphere prevailed through the evening meal,

the athletes not enjoying the waiting game. Most of the individual runners and the teams from the provinces would be traveling now through the night to Nairobi. The budgets of the provincial federations were such that hotels and an earlier more comfortable traveling date could not be afforded. Rose Cheruiyot chose to travel apart from of the cramped bus that transported her Rift Valley team. She thus sacrificed her allowance of $3 dollars!

Back at the camp after a meal of *ugali*, potatoes and beef stew the runners are all in their beds and silence reigns under the canvas. Brother Colm, as usual, would be driving his own vehicle, crammed with runners, to this event. No wonder Colm's last journey to the automobile garage was to have new suspension units fitted!

Some of the runners keep fowl at the camp. They are easy to maintain and provide an income supplement to the wage earned from their employment as servicemen. This is tolerated in small numbers. It is one of these fowls that wakes the camp with a shrill cluck to remind the sun of her duties. Cups of Kenyan tea sweetened past sweetness are swallowed. Many athletes also devour a few bread and margarine sandwiches to sustain them through the day ahead.

In central Nairobi several members of the world press mix with other dignitaries of the athletic domain as they wake up in their respective hotels. A writer for the Boston Globe takes breakfast at the Hilton, one of Kenya's nicest hotels. He has come for the show. The trip will culminate in an interview for their upcoming centennial Boston Marathon with Kenyan favorite Cosmas Ndeti. Ndeti, will not run today's race, preferring to concentrate solely on his marathon buildup.

Around 9:00 hrs the athletes start arriving at the race course. Ancient motorcoaches carry the majority of them. The finish line barricades have been put up and the grandstand is beginning to bubble with excitement, as ebullient fans arrive. The athletes begin warming up. Although the senior men are not expected to begin their race until 11:00 hrs many of them are already jogging, striding out and stretching. Annemarie Sandell of Finland runs alone checking her stride. There has been a lot written about her and her coach, Mike Kosgei, in the newspapers recently and the Kenyans are eager to see how she runs. Stars such as John Ngugi lean on the barriers while surveying the scene, chatting and spinning old yarns with running colleagues. Jos Hermans of the Netherlands, voted the best athlete manager of 1995, wanders about, checking out the talent and his stable of athletes.

**Paul Tergat in the N'gong Hills. Photo by the author.**

Before long the junior girls, mostly barefoot, are in line waiting for the starter's gun. They will run the standard 4km distance. The start is a mad rush to secure a good position. The course
is quite wide though and a good spread of athletes share the fore-
ground. About 80 girls are seeking the first eight places and a
chance to be picked for the national squad training camp from
which the team for the World Championships will be plucked.

Out in the lead with the stride of a gazelle in full flight is
Jepkorir Ayabei, 1995 African junior 10,000m champion. No surprises here. This girl has won every competition over the winter
months and is a hot favorite for a World Championship medal.
Moses Tanui and Brother Colm have been advising her for the
past year. Behind her runs a small group and then a line of athletes that strings back nearly half a kilometer after just the first
two kilometers. If anyone believes that all Kenyans can run, here
that myth is smashed. Girls dressed in school skirts are reduced
to walking, accelerating to a trot as they pass the stands where
the spectators laugh at their efforts.

It is a runaway victory for Ayabei, and all the "big" names
are in the first few places. Brother Colm has a smile from Dubai
to Dublin across his face as most of the girls come from his Iten
training camp. Rose Kosgei, who won this race in 1995, finished
third. The 14-year-old Kosgei has yet to make the World Championships as the IAAF has imposed an age minimum—juniors
must be at least 15 years old to run in the championships.

A brave effort has been made by Jebiwott Keitany, a silver
medalist in last year's World Championships. She had been injured during the last month, limping round Iten the week prior
to the competition, but she was determined to make the effort
here. "I can try; maybe I can make the team." If guts had anything to do with it she would as she was only a few places outside the top eight. Sandell came home a few places further back
in 20th place. She was unconcerned and read less into the result
than the press did. The Rift Valley squad were victorious in the
team result.

Now it was time to test the talent of the junior men. Sparring
each step of the way, 150 runners or so charge round the loop
course like cheetahs after prey. Many drop out, as they give everything entirely to stay with the leaders. Christopher Sogot, one
of Brother Colm's bright hopes for the future, had to drop out
after treading on a horseshoe nail—one of the hazards of using a
horse race track! Two other runners from the Iten training camp,
however, were performing mightily—Paul Ivuti and Charles

Kwambai. Both would eventually be picked for the national squad. Victory went to a relatively unknown Kenyan, Elijah Korir, followed by Christopher Kelong, who had run well in Europe and America the previous year in road competitions. Korir and Kelong represented the Armed Forces and their team took top honors.

Living about 12 kilometers apart, Rose Cheruiyot and Sally Barsosio could find excellent training partners in each other. However rivalry kills those plans, and seldom do these elite athletes meet outside competition. For the trial race to select the Rift Valley squad Barsosio had blasted away only to be caught and passed by Cheruiyot in the final mile or two. Many predicted a similar story for the Nationals. Indeed Barsosio used her usual tactic, and as the gun sounded she was off like a bullet. "Sally is tough, very tough. She tries to run people into the ground. Even if they catch her she won't give in; she'll fight all the way!" commented Brother Colm. Although Cheruiyot hates to lose, her focus was more towards the following week when precious IAAF World Cross points were on offer—she was leading that competition and determined to win it after coming second in 1995.

Barsosio held on to win. Rose scratched and clawed at the distance separating them but never managed to reel Sally in. These two had drawn well clear of the rest of the field even though such names as Pauline Konga, Naomi Mugo and Helen Mutai were in the pursuing pack. Rift Valley Province, with six of the top nine places, captured the team honors. If the teams were purely composed on the basis of birthplace instead of career choices then Rift Valley would sweep all the team results, Moses Tanui reveals. "Yes," he says, exaggerating only a little, "over 95% of the Kenyan team come from Rift Valley each and every year."

Now was the moment all waited for—the senior men's competition. Moses Kiptanui and Cosmas Ndeti were among the celebrity spectators awaiting the race. Jogging to the start in a huge mass were the Armed Forces runners, their flag bearer leading the way. They sang in unison, informing their competitors they were united as a team and ready for battle. It was an impressive sight, no doubt unnerving to the others. Over 250 of Kenya's best cross country runners toed the line. No respect was given to celebrity as each runner had to push for a front line spot. Julius Ondieki, reduced to the sidelines through injury, explained, "Each runner thinks he has a chance at winning, and with the quality of this field if you are left behind at the start then you'll never catch up. They know that!"

Typically it was a middle distance runner who took the lead with all the big names in close pursuit. The first 800m, over rough grass and slightly uphill, was covered in 1:56! The white uniforms of the Armed Forces "A" team soon become prominent at the fore. On narrower courses they will often group at the front and literally block the path of the other runners while their chosen man would spurt ahead of the pack. Josephat Machuka of the Sportsmark team has felt the brunt of such tactics. "Fighting the Army by myself is very tough; they push and block you. If I had a few runners working for me things would be different!"

As predetermined by the Armed Forces coaches, Tergat made his move at eight kilometers. Effortlessly he broke the pack. Joseph Kibor tried grimly to hang onto his shirttails and he would dearly pay. Meanwhile further down the pack established names such as Ismael Kirui, Daniel Komen and John Ngugi were struggling. They would finish 42nd, 50th and 96th, respectively.

Coming to the bell lap after 10km Tergat had strung the runners far and wide, and apparently he had yet to break a sweat. Kibor was still in second, but in the final mile slipped down to sixth. Tergat had only himself to challenge as he collected his third national cross country title. With six runners in the top nine positions the team title was a romp, as usual, for the Armed Forces, and the coaches could breathe again. William Kiptum Mugei took runner-up honors, followed by Machuka who had picked up a slight injury during the race. Fourth place was taken by 1500m specialist Stephen Kipkorir Arusei, a splendid result for him. He backed the race up with a fine 14th place in the World Championships three weeks later and in the summer won the Kenyan national 1500m title and an Olympic 1500m bronze medal. "In Kenya you need 1500m speed to run in the distance races!" he joked, very satisfied with the result.

The awards ceremony was a simple affair. No individual prizes, just certificates, with trophies for the teams. High-ranking Armed Forces officials handed out the awards, and there was a special prize for Paul Kipsilgich Koech—an announcement of a promotion following his meritorious ninth place. The officers were pleased with his service to the team. Lieutenant Koech was to play an important pacemaking role in both the World Cross Country Championships and the Olympics later on in the year, proving his dedication and team loyalty.

The mood after the competition was jovial, laced with relief, at the Armed Forces encampment. The runners seemed very impressed with a runner they knew little about—Julius Bitok. Running for the Rift Valley team, Bitok had slowly worked his way up to fifth place, a result especially pleasing to his coach, the famous Ibrahim Hussein.

A television set was placed in one of the tents so the men could watch the evening news. The report was brief and colorless. The media and public in Kenya are not all that interested in athletics. Football is far more popular.

A feast would be held the next day to honor the victorious teams and the two individual winners. For supper it was the usual *ugali*, potatoes and beef stew, though quite a few runners were adding a bottle of beer or two to the meal this evening. For many of the runners a period of rest would now begin. "Those who have not made the national squad have now finished the cross country season, and the resting period begins before the track training," reports Danny Kibet. "Most runners go home to visit their families."

Sunday morning and all in the Tergat household are celebrating. Many relatives came from Kabarnet, over 300 kilometers away, to watch the Nationals. The three main Kenyan newspapers are opened at the sports section and passed about the room by proud family members, along with photographs taken from Paul's excursions to Europe earlier in the year. Tergat, who is not training today, smiles and has endless cups of tea prepared for the visitors.

As midday approaches the relatives begin leaving for the long trip home. Lunch is a large plate of rice topped with a delicious beef stew. On request Tergat produces a video of the 1995 World Cross Country Championships. "I want to emulate John Ngugi's string of wins," he smiles. Around the room trophies and medals are hung—it is clear that this is the home of a champion runner. In the late afternoon Tergat drives up to the camp to make a guest appearance at the feast prepared to celebrate the heroics of the Armed Forces runners.

The Kenyan Placings in the World Cross Country Championships three weeks later were as follows:

**Junior Women**

| | |
|---|---|
| Jepkorir Ayabei | 3rd |
| Nancy Jepkoech Kiprop | 4th |
| Edna Ngeringwany Kiplagat | 5th |
| Elizabeth Jeptanui | 9th |

Caroline Jepkoech Tarus       10th

Team placing, first. 21 points.
Winning margin of 5 points.

### Senior Women

| | |
|---|---|
| Rose Cheruiyot | 2nd |
| Naomi Mugo | 3rd |
| Jane Wanjiku Ngotho | 8th |
| Sally Barsosio | 11th |
| Florence Barsosio | 15th |
| Lorna Jebiwott Kiplagat | 80th |

Team placing, first. 24 points.
Winning margin of 20 points.

### Junior Men

| | |
|---|---|
| David Chelule | 1st |
| Samuel Chepkok | 3rd |
| Elijah Kipsigei Korir | 4th |
| Charles Kwambai | 5th |
| Gideon Mitei | 7th |
| Patrick Ivuti | 9th |

Team placing, first. 13 points.
Winning margin of 13 points.

### Senior Men

| | |
|---|---|
| Paul Tergat | 1st |
| Ismael Kirui | 3rd |
| Paul Kipsilgich Koech | 4th |
| Joseph Kimani Karanja | 6th |
| William Kiptum Mugei | 9th |
| Josephat Machuka | 10th |
| Stephen Kipkorir Arusei | 14th |
| James Songok | 23rd |

Team placing, first. 33 points
Winning margin of 66 points*.
*Six senior men count for the team score; all other sections count four.

# Part 2
# Profiles of Champions

# Kenyan Pioneers

## Kip Keino

Although neither Kenya's first international athlete or Olympic medalist, Kipchoge Hezekia Keino ranks as one of the most famous and most influential of Kenyan runners. Keino inspired a nation, indeed a whole continent, with his international success. And his post-athletics life has further enhanced his legend.

Keino was the first black African to run consistently and successfully in America and Europe. In the late 60s he became enormously popular with Western track crowds, as he ran with great personality and flair—not to mention great accomplishment.

First seen on the Olympic stage in 1964, Keino finished 5th in the 5000m in Tokyo. It was to be at the shorter 1500m event that Keino would gain true world recognition at the next Olympics. Jim Ryun, record holder in the mile and the 1500m, was the favorite for the 1500m gold in Mexico. Going into the 1968 Olympics Ryun felt he was at a disadvantage however. "Always in the back of my mind remained the phantom of Kip Keino, born and bred in the Kenyan highlands which gave Keino an edge in Mexico City's thin air." If Ryun wanted an equalizer he had more than one to chose from—Keino went into the Games with a gall bladder infection, and in eight days he would attempt the 1500m, the 5000m and the 10,000m events!

The Games began badly for Keino. With three laps to go in the 10,000m he sprawled and lay on the infield clutching his raging stomach. As the doctors approached, he sprung to his feet and rejoined the race to finish last. On medical grounds Keino was advised to withdraw from the remaining events. But Kip had other ideas. No solid food could be eaten; his stomach could only tolerate milk and soft drinks while he rested for the 5000m. In the final he and Mohamed Gammoudi of Tunisia raced shoulder to shoulder to the finish line, with the Tunisian finally edging Kip by two tenths.

Still without solid sustenance Keino prepared for the 1500

**Kip Keino**

meters. "How could I go home failing?" he asked. Keino reached the 1500m finals, running an unencumbered five second faster than he needed to in the heats! Ryun also qualified for the finals as did the German Bodo Tummler who had been all-conquering in the last twelve months.

As the gun sounded Ben Jipcho, Keino's young teammate, shot into the lead. Keino slipped in behind him. Ryun, who was expecting a more tactical final considering the altitude, the distance Keino had already covered in the previous competitions, and the African's infection, lolled towards the back of the field. The first lap was a very swift 56 seconds—3:30 pace! As the world record was then 3:33 surely this was a suicidal pace at altitude. On lap two Keino passed Jipcho and the 800m split was 1:55.3. Tummler was hanging in four meters back with Ryun pursuing a further 15 meters behind.

Still at world record pace Keino strode round the third lap. *Track & Field News* wrote, "He [Keino] was expected to fall flat on his face at any moment." Ryun was now in full flight, but despite a 54 second final lap the American could not catch Keino who won by 2.9 seconds. It was Keino's first victory over Ryun. His 3:34.9 clocking was a new Olympic record. It was to be the fastest 1500 of Keino's career!

On returning to Kenya he was promoted by the Police Department and in the midst of being paraded in the streets of Nairobi Kip fainted from stomach pains. It took six months for Keino to be restored to health.

He returned to the Olympic forum at Munich. In the 1500m final he was passed in the final 100m by the Finn Pekka Vasala, who ran a 1:48 last two-lap split, nipping Keino by a half-second. Six days earlier Kip competed seriously for the first time in the steeplechase event. The Kenyan's style was acceptably ragged but the result impeccable—gold in a new Olympic record!

| | |
|---|---|
| Date of birth | January 17, 1940. |
| Birthplace | Kapchemoiywo Village, Nandi District. |
| Home | Kazi Mingi Farm, 8km outside of Eldoret. |
| Personal bests | 1500m—3:34.9, Mile—3:53.1, 2000m—5:05.2, 3000—7:39.6, 3000 St—8:23.6, 5000m—13:24.2, 10,000m—28:06.41. |
| Height/weight | 5-9$\frac{1}{4}$ (176cm)/143 lbs (65kgs). |
| Honors won | 1968 Olympic 1500m Champion (2nd, 1972) |
| | 1972 Olympic Steeplechase Champion |
| | 1968 Olympic 5000m, 2nd |
| | World record, 3000m and 5000m |

|                       |                                                                                                 |
|-----------------------|-------------------------------------------------------------------------------------------------|
|                       | 1966 Commonwealth Games champion, 1 mile, 3 miles                                               |
|                       | 1970 Commonwealth Games champion, 1500m                                                         |
|                       | Order of the Burning Spear, 1970                                                                |
| Best Achievement      | "My Olympic 1500m gold."                                                                        |
| Family                | Wife Phyllis and seven children, plus "over 70 adopted children at his orphanage on the farm."  |
| Family runners        | Son Martin won NCAA cross country and 5000m title and has begun to be a regular fixture on the IAAF Grand Prix track circuit. Son Bob competes at Arizona. |
| Coach                 | Self-coached.                                                                                   |
| Number of years training | Five years training before international success. Began casual running in primary school.    |
| Occupation            | Director of his own orphanage. Retired Chief Inspector of Police. Professional athlete 1973-74. |
| Training sessions     | Two per day, three in Olympic preparation                                                       |
| Hard session          | 10-15 x 400m with 200m jog.                                                                     |
| Sponsor               | Government help.                                                                                |
| Kilometers per week   | 50.                                                                                             |
| Comments              | To be active in many sports was an important factor to Kip. In the off-season period Keino participated in such sports as volleyball, tennis, basketball and swimming. According to Keino in 1996 his weekly mileage was a mere 50 km, and in some books he has been quoted as running as little as three times per week. Keino's philosophy was to keep quality in front of quantity, not to tire the body with endless kilometers. In training intervals he felt it imperative that the athlete "feels burn" while running. Keino reasoned that unless this feeling was felt in training one could not expect to "run through" such pain in competition. "I had good speed. I could run 21-second 200s. By running lots of intervals I kept that speed fresh. A lot of runners lose their natural speed through too much mileage." |

## TRAINING WEEK

Location: Kiganjo Police Training Centre. Altitude: 2000m. Surface: dirt tracks. Training in spring for the track season.

| Mon.  | AM | 6km steady.   | PM | 5km steady.                                |
|-------|----|---------------|----|--------------------------------------------|
| Tues. | AM | As above.     | PM | 10 x 400m, run in 55-60 sec, 200m jog rest.|
| Wed.  | AM | As above.     | PM | 5km fast/steady.                           |

| Thurs. | AM As above. | PM 15 x 400m, run in 55-60 sec, 200m jog rest. |
| Fri. | AM As above. | PM Hill work. |
| Sat. | AM 5km fartlek or a session of 4 x 800m run in 2 min with a similar rest. | |
| Sun. | AM Long run, 10km good pace. | |

As the competition season approached interval sessions would be adopted. "In the summer I would run many 400m sessions, fast." Although Keino was not renowned for having a great sprint finish he did have excellent speed endurance which was usually enough to wear down his opponents. More often than not Keino ran his sessions solo.

When questioned about Kenyan dominance in distance running, Keino had the following to offer. "The Kenyan runner is free of pressure. Whether he wins or loses over here [in Kenya] it does not matter. They develop naturally. In Europe the young runners are told "win, win" all the time. With no forcing, the athlete enjoys the sport much more. If you have no interest then how can you train hard?"

# Henry Rono

Like Keino, Henry Rono is a Nandi tribesman from the Kapsabet area. Training under the supervision of John Chaplin at Washington State University, Rono made a huge impact on the record book in 1978.

**April 8:** Running the 5000m at Berkeley, Rono claimed his first World record, 13:08.4. The next runner was nearly 50 seconds behind!

**May 13:** In Seattle, Rono ran a startling 8:05.4 to take the world steeplechase record. His closest competitor trailed by over 35 seconds!

**June 11:** In Vienna Rono claimed his third world record, this time at 10,000m. Running splits of 13:49.0 and 13:33.4, he lowered the 10,000m record to 27:22.4. Rono won by the proverbial street—over 30 seconds!

**June 27:** Bislett Stadium in Oslo, Norway, became the next venue for Rono's exploits. The world record in the 3000m was the target. Leading after the first mile (4:04), Rono sped round the last lap in 57.6 second to

**Henry Rono (finishing the world record 5000m at Berkeley in 1978).**

defeat Suleiman Nyambui by over eight seconds! His final time was 7:32.1. Four world records in four different events had fallen to Henry Rono in 80 days!

Henry Rono was to be denied potential Olympic glory by the African boycott of the 1980 Games in Moscow. The subsequent year Rono shaved his own 5000m world record to 13:06.20.

Rono was an impetuous and turbulent trainer, propelling his body farther than many thought was conceivable with training that could amount to three workouts per day, two of which would be high-quality. He virtually wrenched his physique into racing form.

In 1978 Rono ran five sub-28-minute 10,000m races in a single season. He shares this record with another Kenyan, Thomas Osano, who duplicated the feat in 1991. Although it has been many years since Rono returned to the homeland, his *shamba* of over 100 acres awaits in the Eden environment of Rift Valley.

## Ibrahim Hussein

DAVID BENYAK

**Ibrahim Hussein**

The first African to win the New York and Boston Marathons was a Kenyan named Ibrahim Kipkemboi Hussein. Hussein was an economics student at the University of New Mexico and during his stay in America he earned thousands of dollars on the road racing circuit. In addition to three wins at Boston, he also won the Honolulu Marathon three times.

Hussein, who just bought a house in Eldoret (from Peter Rono) and also has a large house just outside Kapsabet, started out as a 1500m runner. Eventually he worked up to the marathon, recording a 2:08.43 best—which was a

Kenyan record in 1988. Today Hussein, although still actively involved in coaching and organizing running athletics, is leaning towards a career in politics. Julius Bitok, Hussein's latest protégé, had one of the best aggregrates in the two qualifying races for the Kenyan national cross country team in 1996. Unfortunately, injury curtailed his season. In November 1996, Hussein was re-elected, unopposed, as chairman of the Nandi District Amateur Athletic Association and also later was elected to the influential position of assistant secretary in Kenya's national federation.

Hussein trained hard! Neither quality or quantity were neglected. Many long road sessions on tarmac were run in his marathon preparations. Long hill runs and intervals were also practiced, as was fartlek. Though he could be out of shape and too heavy for competition a few months before a major race, with extremely hard training—often three sessions per day—he would haul his body into form in a couple of months.

Hussein would regularly run a predominantly uphill route over a tarmac road to his hometown of Kapsabet covering around 22km. "If you work the hills, then running on the flat is easy," reasons Hussein. He also employed tempo road runs of 1 hr - 1 hr 30 min. "Running fast and hard on the roads is the best way to prepare for racing on the roads." Long runs could be up to three hours. "I would often run fast, not much slower than my racing speed." Hussein won over 40% of the marathons he contested.

Mike Musyoki

## Mike Musyoki

Mike Musyoki was probably the most prominent Kenyan road runner of the 80s.

Born in Machakos of the Kamba tribe, Musyoki came to America in 1979 to study at the University of Texas, El Paso. The Kenyan won NCAA titles on both the track and in cross country. Upon leaving the university Musyoki made road running his career. Specializing in distances from 10km to the half-marathon, Musyoki was a prolific winner. He held world road bests at 10k, 15k and the half-marathon. In 1984 his estimated income was projected at $121,000, an amount unheard of for an African runner at the time. Musyoki enjoyed some success also on the track, a surface he found easier to run on than the roads. In the Los Angeles Olympics Musyoki won the bronze medal in the 10,000m.

However as early as 1977 Musyoki had been a prominent force. When fellow Kenyan Samson Kimobwa ran a world record 27:30.47 in Helsinki, Musyoki was runner-up in a swift 27:41.92.

Musyoki trained rather differently than his contemporaries. "I always trained alone," he recalled. "One track session a week, unless there was an important track race." This training was year-round. A typical week:

| | |
|---|---|
| Mon. | One hour, usually 12 miles. |
| Tues. | As above. |
| Wed. | As above. |
| Thurs. | Track session, usually 400s with 60 seconds rest, run in 62-65 sec. |
| Fri. | As with Mon-Wed. |
| Sat. | Race day. |
| Sun. | Rest day. |

These were the sessions that led Mike to a 60:43 half-marathon in 1986.

One could say these runners paved the way for the generation who today dominate the lucrative road scene, as shown below.

### 1995 MEN'S WORLD ROAD RANKINGS

| | | |
|---|---|---|
| 5km | Ismael Kirui | 13:17 |
| 8km | Laban Chege | 22:07 |
| 10km | Stephen Nyamu | 27:09 |
| 12km | Josephat Machuka | 33:50 |
| 15km | Paul Tergat | 42:13 |
| 10 miles | Ismael Kirui | 45:38 |
| Half-marathon | Paul Tergat | 59:56 |
| Marathon | Sammy Lelei | 2:07:02 |

Kenyans all!

And in 1996, on the world's toughest road race circuit, Kenyans dominated, winning every major American road race except Gasparilla, Carlsbad and the Steamboat Classic. After such plums as Peachtree, Lilac Bloomsday, Bay to Breakers, Falmouth, and many more went to Kenyans, Philemon Hanneck of Zimbabwe (the Steamboat winner) lamented, "It is crazy, man! You look around and it is *Kenyans*! I do my best but they are so good."

# Other Pioneers

In addition to the four influential runners  profiled above, mention must be made of other Kenyan "pioneers" who made significant impact on the international track & field scene.

**Wilson Kiprugut**, of course, was the first Kenyan to earn a medal at the Olympics, taking the 800m bronze in Tokyo in 1964; he did himself one better the following Olympics, with a silver in the 1968 800m. Kiprugut also earned a silver medal in the 800m at the 1966 Commonwealth Games.

The first Olympic gold medalist from Kenya was **Naftali Temu**. He won the altitude-affected 10,000 meters in Mexico City in 1968 and also won a bronze medal in the 5000m. He was the 6-mile champion  at the 1966 Commonwealth Games in Kingston. Temu earned two *Track & Field News* #1 rankings—in 1966 and 1967.

**Amos Biwott** started the string of Kenyan steeplechase triumphs with his eccentric victory in 1968. Eccentric because, to the delight of the crowd, he never got wet at the water jump, preferring to launch himself off the barrier completely over the water on each lap. Biwott returned in 1972, finishing 6th. *N.B.* His daughter, Beatrice, followed in her father's footsteps and while attending school claimed a national title in the 400 hurdles.

**Mike Boit** was one of the most popular Kenyan runners of the 70s. His only major international victory was in the 800m at the 1978 Commonwealth Games, but he snared an Olympic bronze in the 1972 800m and was 4th in the 1500. He also captured an 800m silver medal  at the 1974 Commonwealth Games. He had a long career—winning another Commonwealth medal in 1982 (!)— and earned one #1 world ranking (in 1975 when he ran a 1:43.79 800m, just .09 off the world record). Boit is now a busy man, with agricultural interests in the Nandi District, and is an official with the Kenyan A.A.A. He is frequently on the traveling staff at international championships.

**Ben Jipcho** was Kip Keino's 1500m "caddy" in 1968, taking the race out fast for the eventual winner. By the next Olympics he was a medal-caliber runner, earning a steeplechase silver (behind Keino). In 1973 he was *Track & Field News's* Athlete of the Year. That year he broke the world record in the steeplechase twice and also ranked first in the 1500m. In 1974, his quest for a Commonwealth Games triple was thwarted only by Filbert Bayi's world record in the 1500, but he did win the steeplechase and 5000m in convincing fashion. He joined the professional ranks shortly afterward and became one of the aces of that circuit.

**Above left,
Amos Biwott (left)
in the 1968 Olympic
steeplechase final.
Above, Mike Boit.
Left, Ben Jipcho.**

# *The Coaches*

*Few would doubt Kenya's dominance over the past ten years in distance running; and no other country can match their achievements. Behind the "stones" there are always the architects...*

"The coach advises in Kenya; he doesn't rule like a European coach." So spoke Moses Kiptanui.

Middle and long distance running in Kenya can mean big money, comparable to winning the lottery—even mediocre athletes can return home from a racing season with enough money to allow ten years leisure. Coaching is taken very seriously. The job is not well paid in Kenya and the coaches are often "forgotten" by their former athletes when they strike gold, but due to the lure of prestige, travel and opportunity there are many people still wanting to become coaches.

The good coaches are involved mainly for the love the sport. Elliott Kiplimo, a successful Army coach, has been in the game well over a decade and many top runners have been nurtured under his wing, including the late world champion Paul Kipkoech. He has yet to receive more than a sports cap from any of his runners, however. Brother Colm O'Connell has to work a job in order to support his coaching.

Mike Kosgei, after being sacked by the national federation, is now perhaps the most fortunate of the well-known Kenyan coaches, income-wise. This is because he works abroad. When employed by the Kenyan government, Kosgei received a meager salary and a government house to live in next to the national athletics stadium on the outskirts of Nairobi. Danny Kibet, of the Armed Forces, has perhaps one of the best squads of athletes any team could ever muster for distance events. "I have no car and the way things are going the likelihood is I'll never have one either—it is something a coach does not dream of."

Sacrifice is a word often heard in Kenya. The athletes believe that if you wish to succeed then you must put everything into your goal. The coaches follow this approach. Many live in substandard conditions away from their families for months to be with the athletes day and night. "If the runner sees you also are giving all, they will too," noted Albert Masai of the Navy coaching staff.

An important role of the Kenyan coach is as an organizer and a creator of structure. Kenyan athletes are often neither punctual nor organized. When left to their own devices they might reward themselves with a two-week holiday or simply miss training sessions due to other commitments. However when an athlete is plugged into an organized training plan and has someone checking his progress, he or she will give everything and more to training. Brother Colm O'Connell noted how the Kenyans simply enjoy training. "You have to give the European a motive to train. Maybe it is to win a race, or make a team, but with the Kenyans they will train just because they love to run."

In Kenya the personal coach does not exist. Paul Tergat may be the star of the Moi Air Base squad but he receives exactly the same program, advice and help as all the other athletes in the squad. The training sessions are never set up designed to help one particular individual and there is never the one-to-one basis which can be found with elite athletes outside of Kenya.

The system does not work for each and every athlete. Perhaps the great number of athletes hides the failures in this scheme. Mark Wendot Yatich was a neighbor, in Kenyan terms, to the Olympic gold medalist Matthew Birir. Birir was the first to encourage Yatich as a runner. The first important race Yatich ran he defeated a highly talented field including such stalwarts as Simon Chemoiywo, Andrew Masai and Ezekiel Bitok. The unknown runner was immediately recruited by the Moi Air Base team and brought to their training camp. Yatich's form plummeted. The training simply went against the grain for his body. Later he left the camp and reverted back to his old schedule; the results began to pick up.

## Brother Colm O'Connell

The native of Ireland first came to Kenya in 1976 to teach at St. Patrick's High School. He knew next to nothing about athletics. However the day after his arrival Colm attended a track meet and his interest was stimulated. Brendan Foster's brother Peter was in charge of the training at St. Patrick's High School and during the first two years, Colm simply watched and learned. "I depended upon what I saw and observed." This Colm recalled was invaluable as it gave him a perception of the athlete instead of athletics. Twenty years later his walls are full of photographs showing the faces of success.

"I think it is very important to get to know the athlete, to understand the runner. Of course, I spend a lot of time with the runners because they board at the school (Colm's house is on the school grounds). . . My first [top-class] athlete was a chap called Hussein; he [Ibrahim Hussein] won Boston three times and was the first African to win the New York Marathon. . ."

Colm went from success to success. He coached Peter Rono and Matthew Birir, who went on to win Olympic gold medals. Wilson Kipketer left Colm's "stable" to become a world 800m champion. Today no doubt there are others in the wings. Modest, as always, Colm places the credit on the Kenyan mentality. "Kenyans are very responsive to any sort of challenge; it is easy to motivate them. . . The funny thing is that I haven't the qualifications for the job; I would have never have been given the opportunity in England or Ireland."

## *Thoughts From Brother Colm*

"There are three things I don't like for my runners," says Colm "Steep hills, heavy weights and tarmac." For hill work Colm prefers that the runners accomplish a greater number of hill repeats but over a lesser gradient, citing possible damage to the knees. Weights are not found very much in the program. Colm argues that the strength of running comes from running; the exercises that the athletes do without weights, such as sit-ups and press-ups, are ample, he believes.

"Tarmac kills the young legs." Certainly avoiding tarmac in rural Kenya is not a problem and experts have long believed, with perhaps the exception of Arthur Lydiard of New Zealand, that a soft forgiving surface is much more beneficial for training.

Colm talks to the athlete a lot, about a wide variety of things. At his training camp he showed the athletes a movie about racial disharmony instead of the usual athletics video. "I talk more about losing than I do winning," he says. This is not negative talk, far from it, but Colm tries to educate his runners to the realities of becoming an athlete, part of which is accepting defeat, something which Kenyans do with grace and humility in more cases than not. "They know it is only one race, another will follow, and so forth." Analyzing a race is not a subject which appears on

O'Connell's agenda. "It's not a positive thing to talk about problems or be analytical. When the race is over, it's over—until next time."

When asked why the Kenyans are dominating distance events worldwide, Colm offers the following comments. "In Kenya the resources are perfect for running. Long distance running is perhaps the least technical of all sports. You can just go out and do it. In Europe the young adult has many sports to chose from. Not so here in Kenya! Westerners are not as tough as they used to be. Fifty years ago, around the times of the Great Wars, people had to struggle much more; it was a much hardier breed. Now life is easy, but for Kenyans the struggle continues. . . There are very few distractions here in Rift Valley. It is easy to keep a focus on hard training."

Certainly O'Connell is not overoptimistic about the Kenyan athletics set-up. "Kenya is going to have to become more technical with coaching if they hope to compete with the rest of the world. There is a belief in Kenya that if you ignore the problem it will go away, but they are already falling behind. To challenge the Ethiopians we need to look at the new methods of coaching and gather all the information from Europe, but this does not happen. There *is* no information!" Those suffering the worst, Colm feels, are the sprinters. "If the sprinters are not taught from an early age they will never develop the habits needed to challenge on an international level." Another problem is lack of continuity among coaches. "Coaches in Kenya often set off with great enthusiasm, group athletes together and after a short time drop the whole camp."

Is O'Connell different from the Kenyans who coach? Undoubtedly his upbringing has been vastly different. Many Westerners visit St. Patrick's School and a large percentage think, at a glance, that it is a factory that runs itself. These are the people who believe their own preconceived ideas must work regardless of any situation.

No, the successful coach must work from the Kenyan angle, and this is where Colm excels. His understanding, blended with his European planning and efficiency, creates an effective formula. "When death, starvation and lack of medicine hangs on every doorpost it is understandable that Kenyans do not plan or look towards the future."

Peter Rono, Colm's first runner to achieve Olympic gold, is a Nandi from the Kapsabet area. He began by running to school. "Sometimes I would run, sometimes not. With going back to eat lunch I would travel 12km each day on foot. I considered it as just going to school. Now I realize the value," remembered Rono. Asked about Colm's role in his Olympic success Rono was quick to praise his first coach. "Brother Colm is the best coach I've ever had. He encouraged us every step of the way; he became like a father to me. Colm prepared me so I was able to relax in the race. I was so relaxed and that came from the confidence of the good training."

## Mike Kosgei

Who could criticize Coach Kosgei? The man has legendary status among the runners of Kenya. The fact remains that prior to Kosgei's regime, 1985-1995, Kenya had not won the World Cross Country Championships! Ethiopia had dominated with team victories, 1981-85, prior to which Westerners had the upper hand.

"Before I took over, the best Kenyan athletes were not based in Kenya; they were all over the place in Europe and the USA. I brought them back to Kenya. Even today most of the athletes are based in Kenya and leave only for the racing season."

Educated on scholarship at Washington State University, Kosgei competed in track, but not at the level of a Rono or Kimobwa. Injury ended his career but his personal loss became the gain of many others. Discovering an interest in coaching, Kosgei studied for a year and a half in Germany, before taking on a job as an administrator for the Kenyan A.A.A.

A former student at St. Patrick's High School, Kosgei has led Kenya to more gold than the Spanish galleons carried from South America. His approach is quite different from Brother Colm's. "He shouts and shouts at the trackside; he has the eyes of an eagle. There is no slacking when he is in charge of the training," remembered Kip Cheruiyot. "It is no holiday when Kosgei is at the track. He has a knack of seeing if you are not giving everything to the workout, and if you are not—then you're in trouble." says David Keny, a 1500m runner. "Nobody understands the athletes as well as Kosgei; he can make a runner run till he drops," adds John Ngugi.

"The race is planned beforehand with Kosgei; he can tell us how best to win the medals," said Richard Chelimo. Indeed William Mutwol was advised by Kosgei to run hard in the Olympic final of 1992. Mutwol was warned that his finishing pace would be insufficient if the race were slow. Mutwol took the advice and forged a harrowing pace. The result? An Olympic medal, as Kosgei had promised.

Kosgei failed to toe the party line and was dismissed in 1995, following the World Cross Country Championships. Or as one Kenyan newspaper wrote, Kosgei was "dispensed with by Kenya's athletics chiefs for expressing dissenting views." The runners are the real losers. Kosgei was quickly snapped up by a Finnish club in Abo and is working trying to bring the Flying Finns back to standards they once enjoyed in the early part of the century. According to fellow coach Brother Colm O'Connell, Kosgei should not be judged on whether or not he succeeds with the Finns. "It will be tough for Mike; he will be going from runners who can physically manage the training to athletes who possibly cannot handle the work."

# *Thoughts From Mike Kosgei*

"You must train hard, hard, hard! There are no short cuts, if you want to beat someone, you must train harder than he does. Tactics can make a difference but if the training hasn't been done then tactics are of no use," says Kosgei. He is not an advocate of systematic selection. Many times he selected athletes who did not impress in the trials race. Jebiwott Keitany, World Junior Cross Country silver medalist in 1995, was one such case. After failing to finish in the trials for the 1994 World Junior Track & Field Championships, Keitany was devastated. Kosgei saw that it just was not Jebiwott's day. She was included in the squad and won a bronze in the 10,000m.

Another example of Kosgei's insight was brought to the fore after the Kenyan cross country trials in 1996. Sipping a lemon soda in the Nandi Bears Golf Club, Kosgei said that he thought it a mistake not to include Daniel Komen on the national squad. Kosgei was sure that he would perform when abroad, and was he right! Komen took the distance world by storm in the latter part of the 1996 season, ranking first at year's end in the 3000 and 5000 meters.

"All my runners should train and race cross country. It builds strength for any runners. Some runners, if they train for the 1500m, then they are afraid of running 12km cross country races, but that is where the strength comes from. Every runner has speed but you must train for endurance."

Like most Kenyan coaches Kosgei insists on spending quality time with his athletes. "How can you train somebody on the telephone?" he asks. "When you live and breathe with the athletes only then can you make the best of them. . . The coach must oversee the training, be there to push them. The athlete must be pushed to produce his best." The meat of Kosgei's training can be seen by looking at the training of the national cross country team training camp. "There is no magic session, no easy way to the top; it is the culmination of every workout in the week." He likes the week to have a couple of interval sessions and a couple of fartlek workouts as a ground. "Although I have everyone training together the juniors should run around 15% less than the seniors in volume and quality."

Kosgei, the instigator of the large mixed Kenyan cross country training camps, explains why the camps have proved so successful, "I like to have juniors training with seniors and women with the men. It keeps the group alert. The juniors learn much from being with the seniors. They also learn self-belief from training along with the world's best runners. They develop much quicker with this environment." Kosgei also stresses that it is in Kenya where the team bonding takes place. "The runners know how good they all are, so when we race in Europe it is against the other countries and not each other to whom they have to prove themselves."

Flexibility plays a key role in Kosgei's coaching. "It is good to work on flexibility with stretching and light exercises. The more fluid the running action the more economical the running becomes," reasons the coach.

Asked why the Kenyans dominate, Mike gives most credit to the Kenyan character. "Kenyan athletes want to train hard and will train till they drop. They never question the training; they 'just do it!'" chortled the coach. Kosgei prefers his athletes to run fartlek year-round in a controlled manner. "An example of my fartlek? Two minutes full speed with one minute easy, for 30 minutes; the timing should be exact, not 57 seconds rest or 2:05 hard."

Valiant efforts have been made by many Kenyan athletes in an attempt to "win" back their coach. Talks of boycotts have as yet been in vain. Joseph Karatu Ngure, one of the coaches of the 1996 cross country team, express the view that Kosgei is not irreplaceable. "Look at the results in South Africa. Kenya won without him and will continue to do so." Although he has officially "lost" the post of national coach, Kosgei still trains a large number of Kenyan athletes in Nandi District. Undoubtedly he will continue to play a leading role in the fortunes of Kenyan athletics. Kosgei's advice to budding coaches? "Study psychology!"

## Coach Kiplimo Of The Second Rifles Brigade

Educated in England, Elliot Kiplimo comes from Kapsabet in Nandi District. Several months of the year he lives away from his wife and family and is head coach to a group of middle and long distance runners. The winter months he is based four kilometers from Iten in a small camp next to the Kamariny Stadium. "I work for the Army; they fund the camp. We are given a group of runners and are expected to bring around ten per cent to national level." The current best-known athlete in his small squad is steeplechase star William Mutwol. Kiplimo's camp is well respected and the runners are disciplined. Despite his success Kiplimo has traveled abroad (to the World Armed Forces Championships) just once. He owns a small house and little else.

## Thoughts From Coach Kiplimo

"When an athlete comes to me he must give everything to training; otherwise he is wasting my time and his own." Kiplimo does not believe it right to try and persuade anyone to train. He must have the desire before he comes to Kiplimo. "Diet is one part that I teach that a lot of coaches don't. I have studied biology so I understand the role that food plays." Kiplimo is careful to ensure that his runners eat correctly and at the right times prior to competitions. "It is no good eating the correct food a few hours before the race; no, no, that food will not be used anyway during the race. I look towards storing the correct foods as energy in the body," he explains.

Like most Kenyan coaches Kiplimo runs a training program that is not easy. "I believe that training is based upon teaching the nervous system; you must teach them (the muscles) what it feels like to run fast, then faster still." Every day, apart from rest days and days prior to competition, have at least some quality running. "The day before a race I like my runners to stay away from running, but do some exercise—maybe half an hour's strolling, or even some light jogging. It is very important though not to just lie in bed the whole day. This disrupts the sleeping rhythm and makes the athlete feel lethargic."

William Kiprono, one of the better athletes on the team, describes a day of training. "This morning [at 6:00 hrs] we went for 45 minutes hill work. We sprinted up and jogged down a steep grass hill about 200m long. After breakfast we rested before running 5 x 400m on the track. The coach wanted 62-60 seconds. The first we ran 65, then 62, two 57s and a 56. We jogged two minutes rest. This afternoon easy running. I will run around 8km." This training was done at the beginning of the track season. Kiplimo's work load could seem monumental to some. "20 x 800m is a good session for the runners to be doing at the start of the track season.

"Having the camps at high altitude also is a factor that helps us. The good air, the favorable climate and hard working athletes helps me with my job," notes Kiplimo. When asked what makes Kenyan runners different Kiplimo pointed towards attitude and sacrifice. "The runners in Kenya do not question training; they just train. If I tell a runner 'Go and run 20 x 600m' he will, even if he is tired. Also the Kenyan lives for running. Look around this camp—what else is there to do? Nothing!"

# Coaches Albert Masai And Danny Kibet

Living in the N'gong Hills with the Armed Forces runners from October till July each year, Danny Kibet and Albert Masai are in charge of the Navy section of the camp. These two men prepare the team for the Armed Forces Championships. The camp is funded by the Navy but the money is limited. Both men are on serviceman's wages. "We often cannot take a team to races around Kenya because of not having enough diesel for the truck to transport the men. Things like this hold us back." They usually have around 30 men training each day. The most famous of the camp in the 1995-6 season was Shem Kororia who took a bronze medal at the Göteborg 1995 World Championships. Both Kibet and Masai were educated to be athletic coaches.

# Thoughts From The Navy Coaches

"You cannot hope to be a coach unless you fully understand the athlete you are training. This is why it is so important for us to live with the runners," says Masai. He continues, "We hear in Europe of coaches training runners over the telephone and by letters. Ah, they cannot be getting the full potential from these athletes."

"Discipline is strict. I do not want loose morals as they interfere with everybody. Those people must leave the camp," says Masai. "A coach's role here in Kenya is not so much building up a runner; it is preparing a runner," says Kibet. "Kenyans can run but [we can] make them run so much better through a well planned schedule."

"We begin the season in October when the runners come from the military base in Mombasa up to the camp. Mombasa is very hot and not good for training. Then I like to see the runners training 30-40 minutes in the early morning, an hour in the mid-morning at a steady pace and easy running, or strolling in the afternoon. This builds up a base we can work from. Once the runner has the endurance then faster runs take place. After the cross country season is over it is important to take a rest," tells Kibet. "The runners go home for 2-4 weeks to spend time with their family before beginning on the track." Kibet believes rest to be paramount as he thinks the hard training can, if continued too long, cause staleness. "Sundays are also for rest. After a week of hard training the runners need a day of rest to build up the energy for the next week," he continued.

"Can the individual face hardships? Can the athlete live a Spartan life? These are questions I like to be answered by my runners in the affirmative." Masai expect nothing less. The lifestyle is a major factor in success. The two coaches believe it makes the difference between being a national-standard athlete and an international one. "Take sleep—is the athlete prepared to go to bed at nine o'clock each evening or does he want to stay up drinking beer?" asks Masai. "When a newcomer arrives at the camp it is the coach's job to watch carefully to see if this runner will fit in. Kenya is full of young runners coming from the schools, trying to beat the old guard! This keeps our runners on their toes," says Masai.

Belief in themselves is evident when talking to the two men and this certainly rubs off on their athletes. There is no doubting. It is more a question of "If the runner wants to do our work then the results will follow."

# Kapsabet Coach Amos Korir

Patrick Rono, a Kenyan runner who has trained with the Ibrahim Hussein Club, spoke of his training under Amos Korir when he was a junior.

"The base training began with two runs per day—12 kilometers in the morning and eight in the evening. We would do hill workouts, 4 x 800m, with an emphasis on swinging the hands and lifting the knees. After two days of base running we would repeat the hill session, which was very tough and tiring. Once a week we did a long run at normal speed for around 18 kilometers. On that day we would run just once.

"This would last a month before the fartlek sessions would be incorporated. However it was structured 800m, 600m, 400m, 200m and 100m, with the speed increasing as the distance decreased. We would finish with 200m full speed. Taking over from the hill work we would run this session three times a week, over flat dirt roads. The resting time between the efforts would depend on how close the competitions were.

"Next would come the field intervals, 600m x 2, 400m x 2 and 200m x 2, with 200m jog recovery. The 600s would start at 1:35 and speed up to 1:30s. When we were running the field intervals we were told that we should 'feel strong enough to make the sessions okay even though they were tough.' After the base training you had this feeling. The intervals again were run three times a week.

"We were encouraged regardless of ability or form. The coach was Amos Korir and he always had a kind word for us. All diets he told us were good as long as they were plain. Thus those of us who could not afford meat had no psychological barrier thinking that lack of it would affect us. We were advised to drink a lot after the workout was finished."

# 800 and 1500 Meters

National Records 800m:    Sammy Koskei 1:42.28, 1984
                          (Wilson Kipketer* 1:41.83, 1996)
                          Paul Ereng 1:44.84, 1989
                          (Wilson Kipketer* 1:42.67, 1997 WIR)
                          Japhet Kimutai 1:43.64, 1997 WJR
                          Francisca Chepkirui 1:58.1, 1988
National Records 1500m:   Daniel Komen 3:29.46, 1997
                          Noah Ngeny 3:32.91, 1997 WJR
                          Jackline Maranga 4:02.35, 1997
Olympic Medals 800m:      Gold—Paul Ereng 1988, William Tanui
                          1992; silver—Wilson Kiprugut 1968,
                          Nixon Kiprotich 1992; bronze—Kiprugut
                          1964, Mike Boit 1972, Fred Onyancha
                          1996.
Olympic Medals 1500m:     Gold—Kip Keino 1968, Peter Rono 1988;
                          silver—Keino 1972; bronze—Stephen
                          Kipkorir 1996.
World Ch. Medals 800m:    Gold—Billy Konchellah 1987, 91, Paul
                          Ruto 1993; bronze—Konchellah 1993.
World Ch. Medals 1500m:   Silver—Wilfred Kirochi 1991.

*Though Kipketer ran these races for Denmark, his country of residence, he was still a Kenyan citizen at the time.

## Benson Koech

Koech was a star in school as an athlete from Brother Colm's stable. While training for the 800m Koech twice won the junior national and provincial cross country championships—quite a feat considering 1996 Junior World Champion, David Chelule, has never managed to win that set of cards!

"Benson was never really motivated by cross country, though

**Benson Koech**

of course he could have done very well in the Worlds (cross country) if he wanted," said Colm of his fourth(!) sub-1:44 runner.

In 1995 Benson was sidelined by injury and he missed the World Championships, though he did make a return late in the season to win the IAAF Grand Prix final and the overall Grand Prix 800m, beating World Champion Wilson Kipketer. The previous year had been even more promising. Koech was the fastest man over 800m and tenth fastest in the 1500m. To date his only senior medal success came with a silver medal at the World Indoor Championships in Barcelona in 1995, ironically his only indoor defeat of the year.

| | |
|---|---|
| Date of birth | November 10, 1974. |
| Birthplace | Moiben, near Iten. Keiyo tribe. |
| Height/weight | 5-11½ (182cm), 146 lbs (66kg). Racing weight 141 lbs (64kg). |
| Personal bests | 800m—1:43.17, 1000m—2:17.40, 1500m—3:32.90. |
| Honors won | 1992 World Junior Championships 800m, 1st<br>1995 World Indoor Championships 800m, 2nd<br>World junior record, 800m. 1:44.77 (elec. timing)<br>1995 IAAF Grand Prix 800m winner. |
| Home | House and farm in Moiben. During the summer lives in Crystal Palace, London. Training camp location: "Can change"—often Iten with Brother Colm's group. |
| Coach | "Self-coached, but I'm always listening and learning!" |
| Years running | 7 years, 3 at international level. |
| Occupation and faimly | Farmer. Professional athlete. Widowed, with one child. |
| Motivation | "World record or any major championship medal; then consistency! Consistency is what people respect." |

| Training sessions | 3 or 2 sessions daily during the buildup; 2 or 1 in the competition period. |
|---|---|
| Favorite session | Easy morning run. |
| Kilometers per week | 140 maximum, well under 100 in the competition period. |
| Comments | "Listen to your body. Don't run quality sessions if your body is tired. If you keep on with the hard training, you will destroy your form and waste all your training—go back to zero." Koech believes in the block training method, resting between the season's close in September to the new year, "You need to rest to recover so you can start with energy." The buildup begins with distance running, hill running and some gym strength work, "not less than 30 minutes, but no more than 60 minutes, maybe five minutes on each exercise. When the body is weak there is no drive." His tactics in the race: "Always be in the first five places watching. Try not to lead but see if the others can respond if you change the pace." |

## TRAINING SAMPLES

Undulating dirt roads and a dirt track mostly used. Altitude of 2400m.

### April 17-May 18, 1995

| 17th | AM 40 min/11km. | MID 26 min/6km. | PM 28 min/8km. |
|---|---|---|---|
| 18th | AM 30 min/8km. | MID 18 min/4km. | PM Rest. |
| 19th | AM 34 min/10km. | MID 20 min/6km. | PM Rest. |
| 20th | AM 42 min/12km. | MID Rest. | PM 22min/6km. |
| 21st | AM 20 min/6km. | MID Rest. | PM Rest. |
| 22nd | AM 42min/12km. | MID Rest. | PM Rest. |
| 23rd-26th | Traveling about. | | |
| 27th | AM 27 min/8km. | MID Rest. | PM Hill work. |
| 28th | AM Rest. | MID Easy jog, 9km. | PM 18 min/6km fast. |
| 29th | AM 30 min/9km. | MID Rest. | PM 22 min/6km. |
| 30th-4th May | Travel home, rest. | | |
| 5th | AM 45 min/12km. | MID Rest. | PM 24 min/6km easy. |
| 6th | AM Rest. | MID 94 min, hilly long run. | PM Rest. |
| 7th | AM 22 min/6km. | MID Church. | PM Rest. |
| 8th | Rest Day. | | |
| 9th | AM 28 min/8km. | | |
| 10th | AM Easy 6km jog. | MID Rest. | PM Rest. |
| 11th | AM Rest. | MID 5 x 500m, (118 sec x 3, 117 + 115), | |

|      |     |                          |     |                          |     |                          |
|------|-----|--------------------------|-----|--------------------------|-----|--------------------------|
|      |     |                          |     | 5 min rest in-between each interval; |     |                          |
|      |     |                          |     | 2 x 400m (55 + 57), 1 min rest between; |     |                          |
|      |     |                          |     | 2 x 200m (26 + 26), 30 sec rest between; |     |                          |
|      |     |                          |     | 2 x 100m (12.2 + 11.0), 5 sec rest between. |     |                          |
| 12th | AM  | 18 min/6km.              | MID | 6km jog to the track 5 x 300m (43, 44, 43, 42 + 42), 2 min rest. |     |                          |
| 13th | AM  | Rest.                    | MID | Hill work.               | PM  | Travel home.             |
| 14th | Rest. |                        |     |                          |     |                          |
| 15th | Travel, with a little easy jogging. | | |     |                          |     |                          |
| 16th | Evening— 5 x 400m (62, 59, 57, 59 + 59), 1 min rest; 5 x 300m (40, 42, 42, 43 + 40), 1 min rest. | | | | | |
| 17th | AM  | 6km hard.                | MID | Rest.                    | PM  | 1000m + 400m x 2, 1 min rest in between. |
| 18th | AM  | Rest.                    | MID | Rest.                    | PM  | 400m x 3, 2 min rest; 300m x 2, 15 sec rest. |

## July 31-August 10, 1995

|      |     |                          |     |                          |     |                          |
|------|-----|--------------------------|-----|--------------------------|-----|--------------------------|
| 31st | AM  | 40 min very hard.        | MID | 4 x 200m (28, 25, 25 + 24) ; 3 x 300m (37, 39 +39). | PM  | Jogging/strides, 30 min. |
| 1st  | AM  | 30 min jog + light weights. | | |    | PM      | Rest.                |
| 2nd  | AM  | Rest.                    | MID | 3 x 400m (50, 49 + 50)+ 2 x 150m accelerations. | PM  | 28 min + hill work.      |
| 3rd  | AM  | Rest.                    | MID | Light weights.           | PM  | Rest.                    |
| 4th  | AM  | 30 min.                  | MID | 2 x 500m (103 + 102 sec); 2 x 300m (39 + 39). | PM  | 30 min hill work + strides. |
| 5th  | AM  | 40 min fast.             | MID | weights.                 | PM  | Hill work.               |
| 6th  | AM  | Travel home.             |     |                          |     |                          |
| 7th  | AM  | Rest.                    | MID | 2 x 600m (115 + 118), 200m strides (25 + 27 sec). | | |
| 8th  | AM  | Rest.                    | MID | 6km. jog + light weights. | PM  | Short hill, 5 x 20 sec.  |
| 9th  | AM  | 6km hard.                | MID | 4 x 300m (39, 37, 38 + 38). 2 x 150m (15.5 + 16.2, flying start). | | |
| 10th | Rest day. |                    |     |                          |     |                          |

The AM session would be run at 06.00 hrs, the MID run at 10.00 hrs and the PM session between 15.00 and 17.00 hrs.

# Nixon Kiprotich

A Tugen tribesman now residing in Eldoret, Kiprotich has proved to be one of the most consistent 800m runners of the last decade. With about 30 races in the 1:44s or better, Kiprotich has a pedigree of the highest standard. An Olympic silver in the 1992 Games could well have been gold. "Johnny Gray was elbowing me down the homestraight so I couldn't sprint properly." Fighting off Gray, Nixon neglected his blind side where William Tanui strode past to prevail by the narrowest of margins.

**Nixon Kiprotich**

Although winning his semifinal in a quick 1:44.71 at the 1988 Olympics, Kiprotich was well out of the money in the final. He set a hot pace in that race but faded badly to finish last in a woeful 1:49.55.

1989 and 1990 saw victory after victory, culminating in the 1990 IAAF Grand Prix championship. A " stumble" was a "mere" silver in the Commonwealth Games of the same year behind surprise winner Samuel Tirop, another Kenyan, who was running his first (and last to date) international competition. In 1994 Kiprotich picked up a groin strain while competing at Zürich. He is now training for a comeback, hoping to return to top form.

| | |
|---|---|
| Date of birth | December 4, 1962. |
| Birthplace | Salawa. Tugen tribesman. |
| Height/weight | 6-3/4(185 cm), 146-148 lbs (66-67kg). Off season 159 lbs (72kg); really on form—143 lbs (65kg). |
| Personal bests | 400m—45.8, 800m—1:43.31, 1000m—2:16.45, 1500m—3:38.76, 1 mile—4:01.79. |
| Honors won | Olympic Games 800m, 8th + 2nd (1988, 1992) |

1990 Commonwealth Games 800m, 2nd
1990, 1992 IAAF Grand Prix 800m, 1st
#1 *T&FN* world ranking in 800m, 1993
1989 World Cup 800m, 3rd
African Championships 800m1st (1989); 1500m,
   3rd (1989).

| | |
|---|---|
| Home | Two houses in Eldoret. Two farms, Kabernet and Moiben. Crystal Palace in the racing season. |
| Coach | Self-coached. |
| Years running | Since 1985, though ran a little at school. |
| Reason for beginning | "I joined the army; it (running) was what every one was doing." |
| Occupation and faimly | Retired private, Kenyan Army. Professional Athlete. Married to Rose. Four children. |
| Motivation | Olympic games, and winning. |
| Training sessions | Varying from 3 sessions in the buildup to 1 in the quality period. |
| Favorite session | A hard one that has just been finished. |
| Hard session | 6 x 300m run around 37 sec with 1 min rest in between; 10 min rest, then 10 x 200m run between 23/24 sec with 1 min rest. |
| Kilometers per week | 140-plus in the buildup; not so many in the competition period. |
| Comments | "I used to be a front runner—straight to the front and try to hold it. Then I spoke with Billy Konchellah. Billy said to me that because I could run 21 second for the 200m I was using the wrong tactic. I should sit in and wait to kick." Kiprotich won many races using both tactics, a tribute to his strength, though the thought behind Konchellah's idea is certainly a sound one. |

Kiprotich, like most Kenyans, including Benson Koech, believes in taking a yearly break. After the season's close Nixon takes three months holiday before resuming training. "I put on a bit of weight but I quickly lose it with the hard long runs. I run up to two hours wearing both a sweatsuit and track suit (laughs). People always tell me I run too long for an 800m runner." One training aspect that is unique to Kiprotich is his timing. Nixon begins his first training run often at 2 am! Using the headlights of his personal following car he is able to run in the dark hours. These long runs are used up till March along with fartlek. Kiprotich is an exception as he does not compete in cross country.

# TRAINING SAMPLES

Most of the training during the buildup stage is run on earthen roads at an altitude of 2000m. Due to injury problems Kiprotich prefers to stay away from the curves of a track and runs intervals on the straight roads by the new Eldoret Airport. In Kenya training is accomplished individually; however when in Crystal Palace Nixon trains alongside compatriots Benson Koech and Lucas Sang. Stretching does not play a major part in Nixon's training. For a speed runner he gets away with doing an amazingly small amount.

## March 1996

Day 1   Jogging 10km.
Day 2   Intervals     2 x 400m, 5 min rest (48 + 50)
                       2 x 200m, 3 min rest (27 + 26)
                       6km warm-up + 2km warm-down jogging.
Day 3   Jogging, 2 x 10km.
Day 4   Rest day.
Day 5   Intervals,    6 x 300m, 1 min rest (37-39)
                       6km warm-up + 2km warm-down jogging.
Day 6   Jogging, AM  30 min. PM  10km.
Day 7   20km long run.

Kiprotich likes to use time trials to see how his form is. Four days before the 1992 Olympic Games semifinal Nixon ran a solo 500m. Passing 400m in 46 he finished in 58 seconds. "I could still feel that run in my legs in the semi—but I knew I was ready!"

Today Nixon works alongside Yobes Ondieki, Moses Tanui, Patrick Sang and Peter Rono. Along with a large group of athletes in the Eldoret region they are trying to change the Kenyan Amateur Athletic Association. "The officials should be all thrown out," says Ondieki. Nixon comments, "It is hard to fight a powerful organization, but we are trying and putting our own money into it. None of the runners you see racing in Europe have had assistance from the federation. There is money coming in through sponsorship but nobody can see where it is being spent!"

Certainly an ocean of complaints can be heard in Kenya; nearly every runner has his own personal story of dissatisfaction with the federation.

# William Tanui

Success came relatively late to William Kiptarus Tanui, but when it came it was at the highest level—an Olympic gold medal at the Barcelona Games. A year earlier Tanui had won, then lost (due to a disqualification for a lane violation) the World Indoor 800m Championship. Tanui had wavered between the 1500m and the 800m before 1992. African Champion and sixth at the Commonwealth Games 1500 in 1990, he showed promise at the longer distance. But winning the national title and running the second fastest 800m of the year in the same year certainly showed more than competence in the shorter event. 1990 was in fact the breakthrough year for Tanui, as he took four seconds off his 800m personal best, two seconds from his 1500m best and ran an excellent 1000m personal best of 2:15.83, to boot!

After winning the Kenyan 800m Championships in 1992 and thus gaining selection to the Olympics, Tanui came under increasing obligation. "The pressure of being the top Kenyan is terrible; people were coming up to me and telling me that it was for sure that I would win the gold." Kenya expected nothing less than perfection, they very nearly got it, with a 1-2 finish.

The week before the final the stress continued. "I slept barely two good hours in the final week I was so nervous, and the weather was damp with heat." A Nandi from Kobujol, Tanui had dreamt of Olympic glory. "Isn't it every runner's dream?" asks Tanui. The Olympics were his motivation. Now was his chance. Johnny Gray, as Tanui had expected, drew the pace out fast. "I knew if I could just keep within ten meters I would be okay; I did not want to kill

**William Tanui**

myself. . . At the beginning of the second lap I knew I had won the race," William remembers. He had been sure of a winning at least a medal but now he felt gold was his. "Coming down the homestraight. . . it was close, wow." Tanui differs from most Kenyans in the fact that he is a vegetarian—quite a rarity in Kenya.

## TRAINING

A former clerk in the Kenyan Air Force and now a successful businessman specializing in auto imports, Tanui ran and trained with the Air Force runners. Flexibility plays an important role in his training plan, and he typically uses the Kenyan method of light exercising while stretching. "You need good flexibility for your stride to be effective."

Unlike many Kenyans Tanui prefers to stay and train in Kenya the year round, only going Europe when in form for races. "Here [in Kenya] it is perfect."

In 1996 Tanui had intentions of moving to the 1500m, as he felt his sharpness was not as good as in previous years. He adjusted by running more distance cross country training over the winter months to gain strength. "In 1995 I ran 3:33 just off my 800m form (3:33.69 in Monaco). I think I can run well with the extra endurance," he said after completing a 15km tempo cross country run with the Air Force runners. The training paid off. In June Tanui earned himself a berth on the Kenyan Olympic 1500m team and reached the final in Atlanta. Tanui finished a fifth behind teammates Laban Rotich and bronze medalist Stephen Kipkorir.

Tanui was impressively consistent during the Grand Prix season of 1996, considering this was his maiden season as a 1500m runner: Lausanne—3:33.67, Nice—3:35.56, Monte Carlo—3:32.42, Zurich—3:31.20 (PR), Köln—3:33.62, Brussels—3:33.36, Berlin—3:51.40 (PR), Rieti—1:44.55, Monte Carlo—3:39.88 (winner, 3:38.80, El Guerrouj) and Sarajevo—2:16.60. Olympic series: 3:37.72, heat 2nd; 3:33.57, semi 4th; 3:37.42, final 5th.

## BEGINNING OF TRACK SEASON

| Day 1 | AM | 12 x 300m (41-44 sec) with 3 min recovery. | PM | 6km jog. |
|---|---|---|---|---|
| Day 2 | AM | Easy 8km. | | |
| Day 3 | AM | 3 x 800m (1:56-1:59) with 3 min recovery, then 400m flat out. | PM | 6km jog. |
| Day 4 | AM | Easy 8km. | | |

| Day 5 | AM | 5 x 600m (1:24-1:26) with 3 min recovery. | PM 6km jog. |
| Day 6 | AM | Easy 6km. | |
| Day 7 | AM | 12 x 200m (24-26 sec) with 3 min recovery. | PM  6km jog. |

Tanui's Personal Records: 800m—1:43.30; 1000m—2:15.83; 1500m—3:31.20; 1 mile—3:51.40.

# Kip Cheruiyot

One of Kenya's most consistent and prominent middle distance men has been Kip Cheruiyot. Encouraged to compete in athletics at secondary school, Kip soon rose to world standard. As a junior he won the Kenyan national senior championships three years in a row over 1500m and set a junior world record of 3:34.92.

Winning the African 1500m championship in 1982 was Kip's launch into the international athletics arena. The following year he competed in the inaugural World Championships. Although he progressed no further than the qualifying heats it was still an achievement for the junior. Making the Olympic team was a principal goal for Kip, and he managed to achieve this dream in 1984, again exiting in the heats. The World Championships of 1987 saw Kip progress to the final in Rome where he finished 11th. Continuing to improve, he made the Olympic final the next year where he finished a creditable 7th, behind schoolmate Peter Rono who took the gold. As well as winning the World Student Games Championships in 1989, where he took revenge on Peter Rono, Kip also placed third overall in the IAAF Grand Prix, a result which helped to set him up in a modest business enterprise in Kenya.

After his Olympic performance there was interest in Kip from several American universities. Cheruiyot, along with twin brother Charles and Peter Rono, decided on Mount St. Mary's University in Maryland. Charles, born a few minutes before Kip, was the junior world record holder in the 5000m and also a double Olympian. Brother Colm, coach to Kip when he was at St. Patrick's, felt that the coaching system at Mount St. Mary's did not suit Kip and Charles and they never reached their immense potential. "They were both extremely talented natural runners— perhaps more so than any other runners I've coached," remembers Colm.

Unfortunately Kip was badly injured in 1992. Training on the American roads, he overtrained while preparing for the Olympics. "I was training with Ibrahim Hussein and doing his training instead of mine—not good as he was a marathon runner!" The injury dragged on and never cleared up. However, with his twin brother Charles still competing internationally, Kip has not lost the dream yet. "Now even Peter Rono is running well again," declares Kip with a glint in his eye, referring to Rono's European indoor successes of 1996. Maybe the Musketeers of Mount St. Mary's still have some running in them yet!

| | |
|---|---|
| Date of birth | December 2, 1964. |
| Birthplace | Near Lake Baringo. Tugen tribe. |
| Height/weight | 5-5(165cm), 119 lbs(54kg). |
| Personal bests | 800m—1:46.48 (1986); 1500m—3:33.07 (1986); Mile—3:52.29 (1988); 3000m—7:45.80 (1989) |
| Honors won | 1982 African Championships 1500m, 1st |
| | 1989 World Student Games 1500m, 1st |
| | 1983 World Junior 1500m record, 3:34.92 |
| | 1989 IAAF Grand Prix, 3rd overall. |
| Home | Eldoret. |
| Training base | Flagstaff, Arizona, and Cardiff, Wales, were commonly used and liked. |
| Coach | Brother Colm. Also team coaches Kip Keino and Mike Kosgei. "I enjoyed the coaching of Brother Colm the best," says Cheruiyot. "Kosgei was strict, and loud! Colm was more encouraging. He gave us more advice than instruction." |
| Family | Wife and twin daughters Janet and Jacqueline. |
| Years running | "I was encouraged by Charles to take up athletics while attending St. Patrick's Secondary School. I wanted to be a 200m/400m runner but he advised me to try middle distances." |
| Family runners | Double Olympian and ex-junior world record holder, twin brother Charles. Charles, a 3:55 miler, finished sixth in the Los Angeles Olympics 5000 with a personal best of 13:18.41. |
| Motivation | "Brother Colm told me I could be good." |
| Occupation | Agricultural businessman, renting out his Harvester combine. |
| Training session | Often two running sessions and one of exercise per day. |
| Hard session | 5 x 400m, full speed. "Maybe 51-53 second when I trained with the army runners." Run with a 2-minute recovery jog. |
| Kilometers per week | In season, around 70; more in the buildup stage—around 110. |

"When you are tired do not force yourself." Kip means there is no point in grinding the body into the ground as he feels a lot of Kenyans do today. "Try to find conditions that will allow you to train properly and uninterrupted." Moving round the country may be difficult but Kip feels if you want to give the sport your best shot the environment should be carefully considered. "Try to keep to soft surfaces to save the legs." This Kip felt was the reason for his injury. When he trained with Hussein in 1992, he ran every day on hard tarmac roads.

When feeling tired alternative exercises can be used, or if an interval session is planned Kip could substitute a session of grass sprints diagonally across a football field. "Doing something is better than nothing." However Kip feels, "If you skip a day then the following day must be a tough training day."

## TRAINING PLAN

Like most Kenyans Kip believes in the block system. After a couple of months of complete rest the endurance phase begins. "Have a number of different routes. Do not always run the same runs. Vary the tempo also but try to work at improving the times each week." The endurance block should be at least three to four months, ideally cross country training and racing. Fartlek runs are a key ingredient to Kip's training with spurts usually of 600-800m in the forest. "I like to run fartlek in the morning when the air is at its best."

Kip also uses fartlek as a transition tool to move from the endurance phase to the speedwork block. A flexible body is imperative, thus exercises and light weights should be included in the daily program. At the start of the speedwork block Cheruiyot uses time trials for the first three weeks. These are dropped in favor of minor competitions once the season comes into full flow. "It is useful to run small competitions and run at just 85% effort," says Kip. With track sessions Cheruiyot used to run quaility intervals not amounting to more than 3000m. This he felt was enough for a 1500m runner.

A few road races, in the month of May before the European track season, are good for gaining speed endurance as long as they aren't run to the absolute end of the athlete's ability, thinks Kip, though there are no road races run after May and no more than five races total on the hard surface. "When training, it is important to have a good training partner, preferably someone better than you, to push you along. In the cross country season this is not as important as in the track session."

Under race conditions, Cheruiyot felt that it was very important to think about the length of the stride. "This I feel is why [Domingos] Castro failed to catch [John] Ngugi at the '88 Olympics; he used too short a stride when increasing his pace. I think it is better to slowly lengthen the stride when pulling someone back."

Like most Kenyans Cheruiyot thought that if he felt good after 400m in a distance race, then there was no reason whatsoever to wait, regardless of the other competitors' talents as kickers or surgers. "If I felt good after the first lap then I'd go early for the push to the finish."

Cheruiyot had a relatively long career, spanning over ten years at international level. This he feels was helped by sensible racing plans and avoiding the burnout syndrome of too many hard races.

## TYPICAL WEEK

Winter cross country season.

| Mon. | 07:00 | 10km fartlek, with bursts of 400m, 600m and 800m, keeping a good pace in the recoveries. |
| | 15:00 | 8km steady. |
| Tues. | 07:00 | 8km good speed tempo run. |
| | 15:00 | 10km 40-45 min. |
| Wed. | 07:00 | 10km fartlek, as Monday. |
| | 15:00 | 6-8 x 200/300m hill, x 2 jog-down. |
| Thurs. | 07:00 | 8km good speed tempo run. |
| Fri. | 07:00 | 10km 40 min. |
| | 15:00 | 10km 40 min. |
| Sat. | | Competition cross country. |
| Sun. | 07:00 | Fartlek, as Monday. |
| | 15:00 | 8km steady. |

## TYPICAL WEEK

Summer track season.

| Mon. | 06:00 | 6-8km jogging. |
| | 10:00 | 40 min easy, 10km. |
| | 15:00 | Stretching/exercises. |
| Tues. | 06:00 | 6km jogging. |
| | 10:00 | 600m x 2, 400m x 2 + 200m x 2, all with 2 min jog rest. —OR—800m x 3 with 5 min jog rest —OR—5 x 400m, 2 min jog rest. |

|       | 15:00 | Stretching/light weights. |
| Wed.  | 06:00 | 6km jogging. |
|       | 10:00 | 40 min easy, 10km. |
|       | 15:00 | Stretching. |
| Thurs. | 06:00 | 6-8km jogging. |
|       | 10:00 | 600m in 75 sec. |
|       | 15:00 | Stretching. |
| Fri.  | Complete rest. | |
| Sat.  | 06:00 | 6-8km jogging. |
|       | 18:00 | Competition 1500m. |
| Sun.  | 10:00 | 10km 40 min. |
|       | 15:00 | 10km 40 min. |

# Japhet Kimutai

Gaining entry into high-quality competitions is tough nowadays. It's even a more formidable task if you happen to be a Kenyan newcomer, due to the plethora of Kenyan runners and the understandable desire of European meet directors to include home-grown talent in their start lists.

"Promoters are fed up with Kenyans. I have run through the era when meet organizers were crying out for Kenyans, but now the opposite is true," says Patrick Sang.

Japhet Kimutai is one of the current crop of Kenyans who is having a difficult time obtaining European meet entry. As a junior, without an Olympic medal or a world's fastest time, his toughest assignment is to toe a starting line in one of the big Grand Prix meets.

Traveling with a group of his countrymen in the summer of 1995, Kimutai finally got a chance to race. The Copenhagen Games were showcasing a 1000m race for their adopted hero, Wilson Kipketer, and Japhet got an invitation. He got a lot closer to Kipketer in the race than most of the "name" competitors. In the very fast time of 2:17.59, Japhet finished second to the World Champion.

Brother Colm, not surprisingly the man behind Japhet's success, did not even see this result as the season's highlight. In Eldoret's Kipchoge Stadium on the 24th of June (2000m above sea level), on an ankle-twisting track surfaced with loose red cinders, Kimutai captured the schools 800m title. This in itself was not surprising, as he'd been a hot favorite to win. It was the manner in which he won that opened so many eyes. Japhet is a runner with a serious kick. Such runners, as Japhet normally does, usually sit and wait. On this day, however, at the gun Japhet blasted away. He slowed a bit on the second 200m, but reached the bell lap well clear of the field in 49 seconds! Fighting the lactic instead of his opponents, Kimutai finished in 1:46.9, an outstanding time considering the conditions and his 17 years.

**Japhet Kimutai.**
**Photo by the author.**

As a good judge of athletic ability, Brother Colm believes Kimutai combines the best ingredients of two former pupils—Wilson Kipketer and Benson Koech. "Oh, of course it is impossible to say with Kenyans. I have given up guessing who will make it, but Japhet has the guts of Benson and even more smoothness than Kipketer." Kimutai has already surpassed Kipketer's personal schoolboy record of 1:45.7, with a 1:45.63 in 1996.

| | |
|---|---|
| Date of birth | December 20, 1978. |
| Birthplace | Lelmokwo, Nandi District. |
| Height/weight | 5-8 ³/₄ (175cm), 123 lbs (56kg). |
| Personal bests | 800m—1:45.63, 1000m—2:17.59, 1500m—3:45. |
| Honors won | 1994 World Junior Championships 800m, 2nd |
| | 1995 African Junior Championships 800m, |
| |     1st; 1500m, 1st. |
| Home | Boarding school in Iten. |
| Family | Single. |
| Coach | Brother Colm O'Connell. |
| Occupation | Student. |
| Family runners | None. |
| Reason for beginning | "Enjoyed it, and was good at it." A school teacher from Nandi District contacted Brother Colm and asked him to come and look at a "young boy who was beating all the other children." |
| Goals | A junior gold and world record in the 800m, and to run in the Olympics in the future. |
| Favorite session | Intervals of 400m. |
| Tough session | 8 x 300m run in 35 sec with a 2 min rest. |

| Kilometers per week | 110 for cross country, around 70 in the track season. |
|---|---|
| Training sessions | Two per day, three in training camps. |
| Number of years training | Six years. |
| Comments | "Cross country buildup is very important for me." With three months of good XC training Kimutai felt confident that his track season would be successful. "It is important in track training to become relaxed at speed, and for this you must practice high speed intervals... In races if I want to try to win, then it is best to stay between positions 3 to 5; when it is 200m to go, start moving up so you are kicking full speed the final 100m." Like most Kenyans Japhet realizes that sacrifices also play an important role in athletics. "There are some mornings when I am tired, but I know I must get up and train. Sometimes it is very hard." |

## TRAINING PLAN

Japhet never trains with intervals over 1000m in length. As an 800m runner he feels it is not necessary. The total of intervals generally do not exceed 2500m in a single session, underlining the emphasis on speed. After a holiday at the end of the track season, Japhet resumes training in November. From then till March he concentrates on cross country, an event which he sees as a training tool rather than an event in which to perform well. A short holiday after the season brings Japhet into April—and track training. A typical week of track training would preferably include five interval sessions and one day of complete rest.

## WINTER CROSS COUNTRY TRAINING

Location: Iten. Altitude: 2400m. Surface: dirt roads.

| Sun. | AM | Hill run, 10km uphill. |
|---|---|---|
| Mon. | AM | 30-40 min steady run. |
| | PM | 6km, first 3km very fast, last 3 steady. |
| Tues. | AM | 40 min steady. |
| | PM | 7.7km steady run. |
| Wed. | AM | 30 min steady. |
| | PM | 8km beginning very fast, slowing after 3km, fast finish. |
| Thurs. | AM | 30 min steady. |
| | PM | 4km good speed throughout. |

| Fri. | AM | 30 min steady. |
| | PM | 6km fast. |
| Sat. | MID | 60 min steady. |

As with most Kenyans, the usual warm-up and cool-down with jogging and stretching exercises would be accomplished in the afternoon, often with Japhet and his ultra-supple muscles leading the group. "These exercises help to make the running stride smooth," explains Kimutai.

## SPRING TRACK TRAINING

| Mon. | AM | 6km easy. |
| | PM | 3 x 600m (1:35) + 3 x 200m (25 sec). 2 min rest after the 600s + 1 min rest after the 200s. |
| Tues. | AM | 6km steady. |
| | PM | 8 x 300m (35 sec), with 2 min rest. |
| Wed. | AM | 6km steady. |
| | PM | 7.7km hilly, fair speed. |
| Thurs. | AM | 6km easy. |
| | PM | 10 x 200m (25 sec) + 2 x 400m (58 sec). 2 min rest. |
| Fri. | AM | 6km easy. |
| | PM | 2 x 600m (1:30) + 2 x 400m (58 sec). 1 min rest. |
| Sat. | AM | 5 x 400m (57 sec) + 2 x 200m (27 sec). 1 min rest. |
| | PM | Short hill intervals. |
| Sun. | | Rest. |

Often a warm-up jog would be extended to 4km for the track sessions as this is the distance from St. Patrick's High School to the Kamariny track where the Iten runners do their workouts.

# The Steeplechase

| National Record: | Bernard Barmasai 7:55.72 WR |
| | Paul Kosgei 8:07.69, 1997 WJR |
| Olympic Champions: | Amos Biwott 1968; Kip Keino 1972; Julius |
| | Korir 1984; Julius Kariuki 1988; Matthew |
| | Birir 1992; Joseph Keter 1996. |
| World Champions: | Moses Kiptanui 1991, 1993 and 1995; Wilson Boit 1997. |
| Track & Field News #1 Rankings: | Biwott 1968; Keino 1972; Ben Jipcho 1973; Henry Rono 1978; Korir 1984; Kariuki 1988; Peter Koech 1989; Kariuki 1990; Kiptanui 1991-1995, 1997; Keter 1996. |

The Kenyan record of success is obvious in all running events, 800m through the marathon, but it is in the steeplechase that Kenyans have truly been dominant. Kenyans competed for six Olympic steeplechase titles since 1968 and won all six. Moses Kiptanui, the world record holder, has taken the gold medal at the last three World Championships. Kenyans have won all the Commonwealth Games steeplechase golds since 1974, except for Edinburgh (1986) when the Kenyan team joined a boycott against the Games. Kenyan athletes have been #1 ranked in the steeplechase since 1988. In 1996, Kenyans placed 9 out of the first 10 in the rankings, missing only place #7. The previous several years show similar dominance. This is truly "the Kenyan event."

Why are Kenyans so exceptional in this event? Purists frequently cringe as many of the Kenyans "hurdle" the steeplechase barriers. Kip Keino joked that he jumped the hurdles like an old horse. Patrick Rono, a national standard runner, thinks he has the answer. "A group of us were sitting watching a local competition one day. . . A British runner was over here in Kenya running against us. We noticed first the big difference in leg structure; his legs were like oak tree trunks whereas ours were like willows. When we jumped we floated over; when he jumped it was a major upheaval." Though willow-like legs are not the exclusive property of Kenyans, perhaps Rono does have a point. The Kenyans do seem to skip over the hurdles with ease, regardless of form, and this conservation of effort could be a key to Kenyan steeplechase success. Many have criticized the Kenyans for their seemingly ungainly style of clearing obstacles, but style marks are not needed to win this event.

Kirwa Tanui, a steeplechaser, speaks of the Kenyan belief in themselves. "A lot of Kenyans choose to run the steeplechase event because we know we are unbeatable; maybe we have some doubts in the 5000 or the 1500—we know that Kenyans are often beaten in those races. But when we run the steeplechase, we know that we shall win—no problems!"

King of the barriers is a title surely held by Eldoret resident **Moses Kiptanui.** The world's first and to date only sub-8-minute steeplechaser, Kiptanui was a hot favorite to win the 1996 Olympic title. In 1995 he had won his third consecutive World Championship and had demolished the world record, lowering it to a fantastic 7:59.18.

The Atlanta final was to cap his career. In Kenya he had talked of retiring and this was the one laurel missing from his cabinet. Kiptanui bided his time, running near the front much of the way, but a virtually unknown teammate Joseph Keter was to choose this race as his break-through. With 300m remaining, the two Kenyans unleashed their kicks and Keter—shocking the crowd—proved the stronger this day. Keter won in a fast 8:07.12, more than a second ahead of the world record holder.

The Olympic silver was a great disappointment to Kiptanui, but it hardly tarnishes a great career. Kiptanui is another formidable Kenyan trainer. When questioned about his favorite sessions, Kiptanui had the following to offer: "I like to run up a mountain we

**The great Moses Kiptanui.**

have near Nyahururu. Track sessions such as 8 x 400m in 55-57 seconds, or 12 x 400 in 59s, and 800m in 1:57/8 are good work-outs. The main thing is *effort*. Training must be tough, very tough!" These workouts are run at high altitude.

Jackton Odhiambo, who trained alongside Kiptanui in 1995, remembered the sessions he shared with Moses. "We would run 20 x 400m at the Kipchoge Stadium in Eldoret. We were to jog 200m between each interval. Moses led every interval and turned the jog rest into a 100m jog. Nobody could keep up with him. It was the same in every training run, on the track or off! Nobody was surprised when Kiptanui had such a good season in Europe that year." According to Jackton he saw Moses do a 3000m time trial training session in an amazing 7:37 on the Eldoret dirt track!

"I don't train so much over the barriers. I train with 1500m to 10,000m runners—we all do the same training. Running in the country builds strength for the steeplechase." Olympic bronze medalist William Mutwol.

"There is no secret to our success in the steeplechase. To be com-petitive in the steeple today you have to be able to run a 5000 in around 13:15, but in most countries if you run 13:15 you are a 5000m runner—not in Kenya!"Bernard Barmasai, an 8:08.56 steepler.

"I train often with Ismael Kirui. We do the same training but com-pete in different events. . . I do no specific steeple training." Chris-topher Kosgei, 1995 World Championships silver medal winner.

"Cross country training and running over the hills is the best preparation for running the steeplechase event. Good strength is very important. Run hills often." Julius Korir, 1984 Olympic Champion.

# *Patrick Sang*

Every year a new batch of East African athletes appear on the world athletics stage. Even the most senior Western observer cannot identify half the Kenyans in a steeplechase event. How-ever one veteran has been in the picture for over a decade and is well-known to all track aficionados—Patrick "Silver" Sang.

In 1987 Sang won the All-African Games and reached the final of the Rome World Championships, finishing eighth. The following year Patrick "ran stupidly" to finish 7th in the Seoul Olympics. Watching the video years later Patrick is quick to identify his inexperience.

In 1991 Sang collected a silver medal at the Tokyo World Championships behind Moses Kiptanui. It had been his goal to medal at these championships, and he succeeded.

The Kenyan trial race for the three steeplechase spots for Barcelona in 1992 was held in Nairobi. The lineup was one of the finest fields ever assembled. Peter Koech, fresh from a training camp in Spain and the reigning world record holder was in majestic form. Julius Kariuki, the defending Olympic champion and Olympic record holder, was running very well and so was the World Champion from the previous year, Moses Kiptanui—a favorite in the eyes of many. None of these superb runners made the team.

Matthew Birir, a St. Patrick's student, ran a sensational 8:12 at an elevation of 1600m to win, followed by Sang and William Mutwol. These three runners then trained together for a month before the Olympics and a bond was forged. Running as a team they swept the medals. "I took the pace out because that was my strong point," recollects Mutwol. Sang adds, "If you watch the replay of the race you can see Matthew and me looking

ALLSPORT/GRAY MORTIMORE

**Patrick Sang—victory in Berlin, 1993.**

back on the last lap to check that William was all right. We weren't going to leave him." Sang justified his selection with the silver medal.

The following year Patrick won the IAAF Grand Prix steeplechase title and another silver medal, behind Kiptanui, at the Stuttgart World Championships. During the 1995 season, Sang ran under 8:10 six times. This included an outstanding 8:08.11 in London, a British all-comers record, and an 8:06.80 in Monaco.

Team captain for both the Olympics and the World Championships Sang commands great respect among his fellow athletes. He has friends around the globe and is an ambassador for both the sport and Kenya. Many athletes have been helped by Patrick's generosity, for instance the young runner from Kapsabet, Geoffrey Tanui. Patrick paid and set him up to be able to run and compete in Switzerland. In the spring of 1996 Sang gave out hundreds of pairs of athletic shoes to the runners of Kenya. A true Good Samaritan of the sport.

| | |
|---|---|
| Date of birth | November 4, 1964. |
| Birthplace | Kapsisiywa, Nandi District. |
| Personal best | 3000m St—8:06.03, 1500m—3:44.17, 2000m—5:03.46, 3000m—7:49.05, 5000m—13:34.95. |
| Honors won | 1992 Olympic Games 3000m St, 2nd |
| | World Championships 3000m St 1991, 2nd; 1993, 2nd |
| | 1987 All-African Games 3000m St, 1st |
| | IAAF Grand Prix 3000m St: 3rd, 2nd, 2nd, 1st (1988, 1990, 1991, 1993) |
| | 1989 World University Games 3000m St , 1st. |
| Height/weight | 5-10³/₄ (180cm), 143 lbs (65kgs). |
| Home | Eldoret and Nandi Hills. In summer based just outside Zürich. |
| Family | Wife Joyce and son Kipruto. |
| Sponsor | Adidas, since 1987. Sang also is his own manager. Competes for LC Zürich. |
| Coach | Self-coached. |
| Years running | Began to train seriously in 1983. |
| Reason for beginning | To gain an American scholarship. |
| Occupation | Professional runner and successful businessman dealing in property and goods. |
| Training sessions | Two per day. Never three. |
| Favorite session | "The ones I've completed that were tough." |
| Hard session | 3 x 1km run at 2:30 per km. |
| Best achievement | A progression of events beginning with first making the national team. |
| Kilometers per week | Around 100. |

| | |
|---|---|
| Training partners | Most often a solo trainer but does run with a group depending on location. |
| Toughest training partners | Yobes Ondieki and Moses Kiptanui. |
| Comments | "Try to be focused." Every year Sang had a high work load at university his athletics suffered. "Working on a thesis until 2 am does nothing for your athletics!" remembers Patrick. "Run cross country races. The years I've trained and raced cross country I've always had a good season in the summer. . . Eat properly, even if it means turning down dinner invitations." Patrick believes in training alone. "Then you run your own session and know where you are. It is too easy to get sucked into running other people's sessions when training in a group. Patrick feels that speed endurance is one of the main keys to success. "I've experimented. After a layoff I can go out and run a good set of 400m repeats, but I cannot run a good set of 2000m repeats. They need constant work." A theory that probably holds true for most runners. |

## TRAINING PLAN

After a holiday during October and November, Sang begins his endurance phase. Two runs per day except for Sunday, when one long run is undertaken. Patrick rests one day in every ten. This changes in the summer when a rest day comes once a week. Specific event training, in Patrick's case hurdling, is done in late April and the beginning of May, just before the track season. From March to May the toughest training takes place. "I begin running 2:50 per km repeats and work down to 2:30s in May with a 5 x 1km session," says Patrick.

In April Patrick moves to his base in Europe to be away from distractions and concentrate solely on athletics. He tests his form in April to see what shape he is in. "I can predict what I can run; this is because I train alone and I know my body. It surprises people that I can predict my race times. If I run 10 x 400m with 60 seconds rest in 60 seconds for each interval then I know I am in form!"

# TYPICAL WEEK (MARCH)

| Sunday | AM | Long Run, 1 hr 40 min on an undulating dirt road at a hard pace. A variant could be a road run predominantly uphill for 22km—a tough run climbing to around 2300m altitude. | | |
|--------|----|-----|----|----|
| Monday | AM | 10km in 40 min. | PM | 8km 32 min. |
| Tuesday | AM | 5 x 1000m with 90 sec rest in between. | PM | 8km easy. |
| Wednesday | AM | 10km 40 min. | | |
| Thursday | AM | 10 x 400m, with 60 sec rest in between. | PM | 8km easy. |
| Friday | | Rest day. | | |
| Saturday | AM | 10km 36 min. | PM | 10km 38 min. |

## A DAY IN THE LIFE OF PATRICK SANG

Patrick Sang's neighborhood perches on the outskirts of Eldoret. To the left of the Sangs' spacious bungalow, some distance up the road, is the house of the first man to run a sub-27-minute 10,000m, Yobes Ondieki. Ondieki built this house with his ex-wife Lisa. The vast expanse of land that envelopes the large Ondieki house gives the homestead a majestic setting. About half a kilometer down the road from Sang lives another 10,000m star, Moses Tanui. His house, which is hidden from the road, is home to an array of trophies from every corner of the globe. Many vehicles are parked in his compound and building is in progress for a new house on the large grounds. A stone's throw up the road is where Nixon Kiprotich and Kip Cheruiyot live. Quite a neighborhood for training partners.

Dressed in shorts and a t-shirt, Patrick Sang padlocks his gate and prepares for the morning's run. In addition to the bungalow, there are other buildings on the grounds, a large guest wing and a cultivated garden. The crops provide fresh and chemical-free food for household consumption. The family also keeps fowl for the eggs, and what they cannot eat they sell to a local store. Some eggs are reserved daily to be transported to Patrick's general store in Nandi District.

Patrick settles immediately into a steady pace that he will hold throughout the run. He keeps to the sides of the tarmac road trying to stay on the loose gravel verge for a more forgiving surface. The road meets the road to Kapsabet, the center of Nandi District, where Wilson Kipketer, Henry Rono, Ibrahim Hussein, Peter Koech and Peter Rono have homes. Championship medals are as common as trees in Kapsabet.

Today Sang has no plans to run towards his own home district. A red dirt road to the right leads off onto one of his favorite routes. The road undulates, swinging to the left then to the right. A group of Kenyans dressed in their Sunday best wave and shout jokingly to the runner. They are on their way to church. Patrick smiles and retorts good naturedly before his stride has taken him out of earshot. To the right in the distance are the suburbs of Eldoret, to the left the rough countryside with sporadic signs of habitation in the form of wooden or mud huts. After 50 minutes or so, Sang comes to a tree—his turnaround point. The pace is uncannily even, probably around 5:30 for each passing mile, certainly nothing taxing for a man who can hold his own with the world's best middle distance men.

At the end of the workout, Sang jogs to a halt and moves into a series of easy stretches. A white Toyota pickup, one of three vehicles that Patrick owns along with a motorbike, lends its frame to the hamstring stretches Sang uses. His muscles must remain supple over the training season for efficient clearance of the steeplechase barriers.

Breakfast is prepared and waiting on the veranda. Showered and with the daily newspapers, Sang sits down to a cup of Kenyan *chai*, fresh fruit, bread and jam washed down with juice, and to the peace and silence this neighborhood provides. Kipruto, Patrick's spirited young son, has left earlier for church with a girl who helps the Sangs with household chores. Patrick's wife, who works in Eldoret during the week, is elsewhere in the house. After nearly completing the crossword, Patrick clears away the table and welcomes Kipruto home. Sundays are family days for Sang and he regards the time spent with Kipruto as precious. Shortly after midday, Patrick takes an hour or two of sleep, a luxury he can rarely afford during the week when business and training fill the hours,

At half past two a carload of visitors arrive at the house, relatives from Nairobi stopping in for lunch. The table overflows with guests and food. Goat meat stew and rice with vegetables make up the main course. Fresh Kenyan pineapple serves as desert. News of the family is the principal topic of conversation. Although the Sangs have a telephone, most families do not. Sending letters is not that common either, so family gatherings are never lacking in words! Patrick retires to the living room and here one can see that this is a home of an athlete. Most of Patrick's trophies are in his second house in the Nandi Hills, but here one can see a wide selection of metal from world-class competitions.

As guests leave, others arrive. A college friend has just driven in from Mombasa. The role of host is courteously adopted by Patrick, a man popular for many more reasons than his athletic success.

A light evening run of 10km is on the day's menu. The loop begins with a stretch of flat road. Patrick wears a blue fleece track suit. A young lady carrying a sack of vegetables runs alongside the Olympian to Sang's great amusement. The pace of 6:00 to the mile again hardly raises the pulse of the con-

**Patrick Sang and son Kipruto.**
**Photo by the author.**

ditioned runner as he skips over the loose stones of the dirt road. Eldoret has played host to a large agricultural show over the weekend, and the crowds spill out onto the roads as Patrick slips by. Nobody recognizes "Silver" Sang, however. In Eldoret it is more of a rarity if you are a runner *without* world-class credentials!

The run is finished at the same pace at which it began. The more established runners in Kenya seem not to subscribe to the philosophy which demands an all-out race the last mile back home. Straight to the shower and the stretches are left to another day. The schedule has been disrupted by the crush of visitors.

Kipruto is beginning to get tired. The night before he had stayed up too late watching television. He waits for his father to change into casual clothes before the evening meal. One of Patrick's favorite meals is served in the dining room—*ugali* and green vegetables, basic but beautiful in the eyes of most residents of rural Kenya. Kipruto says grace; he thanks God for delivering him and his father safely from a taxi ride they took the previous day, and the meal starts. A cup of *chai* ends the day while Patrick flips through a batch of faxes concerning his summer racing schedule. As he acts as his own manager, all this and much more must be planned before the trip to Europe which he will be taking in a week's time. Bedtime is around 21:40, and tomorrow begins another day of training and, as it is Monday, he has a hundred and one business tasks to attend to.

# *Charles Kwambai*

In the Kenyan countryside, many small villages abound. Often miles from the nearest large town and without electricity, the people are bred tough and strong. It is at one of these villages that the runner Charles Cheruiyot Kwambai spent his childhood.

A former student at St. Patrick's High School, Kwambai looks likely to carry the flame of the Iten school's honor. Charles does not stand out in training. Observing the daily sessions one might just notice that this runner is usually not at the front of the pack, but when it comes to racing . . . then it is another story.

Charles Kwambai's breakthrough came in 1995. After winning the Kenyan schools cross country title in the spring, he went on to win the African Junior championships titles in the 3000m steeplechase, the 5000m and the 10,000m—all run over the same weekend!

A trip to Norway in the summer gave Charles his first taste of European life. Returning a little richer, and with a road 10km time of 29:07, Kwambai had motivation for the winter training season—he wanted another bite!

The hard work seemed to pay off. Charles came in third in the Keiyo District junior cross country championships, and now came the hard part—the qualifying race for the Rift Valley Provincial team. As a runner in Kenya, if you can make the Rift Valley junior men's team you'll have an excellent chance of making the national squad. Kwambai unfortunately had a bad run. Whereas most of the juniors opted to run barefoot on the Nandi Hills course, he chose to wear spikes. The shoes gave him problems and he finished well back. Luckily for Charles, his coach, Brother Colm, realizing that he genuinely had a disastrous run, decided to pay Charles's fare and board for the nationals in Nairobi out of his own pocket and he entered Charles as an individual.

It is said that the Kenyan cross country nationals is the toughest event in athletics. It is hard to imagine Daniel Komen, coming in 50th place, but it is true—only in the Kenyan nationals!

Kwambai proved that Brother Colm's faith was well placed with an eighth position in the junior race. A week later, before the running of the IAAF World Cross Challenge in Nairobi, Kwambai finished fifth in the accompanying junior men's event. The ticket to South Africa and the World Cross Country Championships had been earned.

The night before the World Cross Country Championship race the athletes were given the sponsor's shoes by their team managers. The junior team received spiked running shoes for sprinters. Kwambai tried the shoes and had difficulty trying to run as this model forced a complete change in running style. With a large sandy section to run over Kwambai did not want to risk running barefoot, so he saddled himself with the sprinter's shoes.

Kwambai held third most of the race, but near the finish he was passed by two teammates. Charles finished an excellent fifth behind three of his teammates and an Ethiopian. "Sure, it was good. I thought I could win. At the training camp I was winning all the test races but Chelule [the race winner] was too strong."

| | |
|---|---|
| Age | 17 yrs. old (1996). |
| Birthplace | Kapchelal Village. Keiyo tribe. |
| Height/weight | 5-4¼ (163cm), 115lbs (52kg). |
| Personal bests | 3000m St—8:40, 5000m—13:39, 10,000m—29:37. Set at high altitude on dirt tracks. |
| Honors won | 1995 African junior champion: 3000m St, 5000m and 10,000m |
| | 1995 Kenyan schools cross country champion |
| | 5th place, World Junior Cross Country Championships, 1996 and 1997. |
| Coach | Brother Colm. |
| Sponsor | British athlete Allison Wyeth pays school fees. |
| Years of running | "I began as a small, small boy, running everywhere." |
| Reasons for beginning | "I loved to run, to lead, to be in front." |
| Occupation | Student. |
| Family runners | None. |
| Training partners | Iten Club, made up of St. Patrick's students and local residents such as Rose Cheruiyot and Benson Koech. |
| Training sessions | Two per day; three while in training camps. |
| Favorite session | Tempo running. |
| Hard session | Intervals. |
| Motivation | To help his family. |
| Kilometers per week | 130/140. More when free from school in hard training. |

| Comments | "You must be focused and face self-sacrifice. When the other students go home on holidays I must first think of training. When the race is over [the main goal for the season] then I can relax and go home. It is important to have good support as a runner. Before I came to St. Patrick's I had nobody, no shoes or anything. Brother Colm has helped me much. When I used to run barefoot on the track, my feet would blister so I couldn't train afterwards for weeks! . . . I like to run with a group, watch the other runners, then when they are tired, push hard and leave them behind!" Kwambai clearly encompasses the ideology of running free. |
| --- | --- |

## TRAINING WEEK

Winter Cross Country Training. Location: Iten. Altitude: 2300m. Surface: dirt road.

| Sun. | AM | Hill run, 10km uphill. |
| --- | --- | --- |
| Mon. | AM | 45 min, including a fast 15 min uphill stretch. |
| | PM | 6km race tempo, undulating cross country route. |
| Tues. | AM | 45 min, as with Monday. |
| | PM | 9.6km cross country, steady start, full speed after 10 min. |
| Wed. | AM | 45 min, as with Monday. |
| | PM | 8km cross country, steady start, full speed after 10 min. |
| Thurs. | AM | 45 min, as with Monday. |
| | PM | 7.7km cross country, undulating as usual. Steady pace. |
| Fir. | AM | 30 min easy run. |
| | PM | Travel to Nairobi. |
| Sat. | AM | Nationals, 8th. |

The above schedule is typical for Kwambai for Sunday through Wednesday during the cross country season. Usually the hard efforts would run throughout the week without the tapering. The nationals, of course, was a major goal for the season.

Charles views competitions as hard training sessions. Preceding each of the afternoon sessions, and again as a cool-down, Kwambai jogs for around 10 minutes and stretches with exercises for another 15 minutes.

No specific training is undertaken for the steeplechase event. Charles believes that running over the typical Rift Valley terrain, where one must chop and adjust the natural stride to avoid stones,

**A steeplechase competition at Eldoret's Kipchoge Stadium.**
**Photo by the author.**

bushes and branches, provides him with hip strength needed to clear the barriers in the steeplechase. "Just run cross country over real demanding ground," advises the athlete.

### TRAINING WEEK

Spring Track Training. Location: Iten. Altitude: 2300m. Surface: dirt road and dirt track.

| | | |
|---|---|---|
| Sun. | AM | 40 min steady. |
| | MID | 4 x 400m (58-62 secs), 2 min rest. |
| | PM | 30 min steady. |
| Mon. | AM | 40 min steady. |
| | MID | 4 x 400m, as Sunday. |
| | PM | Easy running. |
| Tues. | AM | 40 min steady. |
| | MID | 7.7km tempo run. |
| Wed. | AM | 50 min good pace group run. |
| | MID | Hill repeats. |
| | PM | Easy running 30 min. |

| Thurs. | AM  | 40 min steady. |
|--------|-----|----------------|
|        | MID | 10 x 300m + 3 x 100m. |
|        | PM  | Some short sprints interspersed with jogging on a grass field. |
| Fir.   | AM  | 40 min steady. |
|        | MID | 10 x 200m, around 30 sec, with a minute rest. |
|        | PM  | 30 min easy. |
| Sat.   | AM  | 35 min fast. |
|        | PM  | 5 x 400m. |

If Kwambai feels that the training is beginning to wear him down physically he is not afraid to rest up for a few days before resuming training again.

A born natural runner, Charles thrives best on natural training. "When I was a child and running to school, or on an errand, sometimes other children would run with me. I would try and run from them. I loved to see people behind me when I ran as a child." Covering vast distances at a tender age Charles ran about 10km to school, back for lunch, back again and home in the evening—a staggering 40km per day. Even allowing for possible exaggerated distance, the base Kwambai must have built up is certainly now paying its dividends.

# 5000 and 10,000 Meters

| | |
|---|---|
| *National Records 5000m:* | Daniel Komen 12:39.74, 1997 WR |
| | Philip Mosima 12:53.72, 1996 WJR |
| | Rose Cheruiyot 14:46.44, 1996 (9th all-time) |
| *National Records 10,000m:* | Paul Tergat 26:27.85, 1997 WR |
| | Richard Chelimo 27:11.18, 1991 WJR |
| | Sally Barsosio 31:32.92, 1997 WJR |
| *Olympic Medals 5000m:* | Gold—John Ngugi 1988; silver—Kip Keino 1968, Paul Bitok 1992, 96, Pauline Konga 1996; bronze—Naftali Temu 1968. |
| *Olympic Medals 10,000m:* | Gold—Temu 1968; silver—Richard Chelimo 1992, Paul Tergat 1996; bronze—Mike Musyoki 1984, Kipkemboi Kimeli 1988. |
| *World Ch. Medals 5000m:* | Gold—Yobes Ondieki 1991, Ismael Kirui 1993, 95, Daniel Komen 1997; bronze—Shem Kororia 1995, Tom Nyariki 1997. |
| *World Ch. Medals 10,000m:* | Gold—Paul Kipkoech 1987, Moses Tanui 1991, Barsosio (W) 1997; silver—Chelimo 1991, Tanui 1993, Tergat 1997; bronze—Chelimo 1993, Tergat 1995. |

## Training For The 5000/10,000m

**Moses Tanui** can be called upon as an authority on distance running with a World Championship 10,000m gold medal in his cabinet! "When training for the 5000m and 10,000m speed has to be remembered." Here's a sample training week.

Mon.   One session of easy running and one of intervals, 5 x 2000m with 3 min jog rest. Finish the session, as with all interval sessions, running 5 x 200m flat-out to keep your finishing

|        | speed in order. |
|--------|-----------------|
| Tues.  | One session of easy running and another of medium-to-hard running over 60 minutes. |
| Wed.   | One session of easy running and one of intervals, 20 x 400m with 1-2 min jog rest. Plus the 5 x 200m for speed. |
| Thurs. | Two sessions of about one hour duration, one easy and the other at a medium pace. |
| Fri.   | The same as above. |
| Sat.   | One session of easy running and one of intervals. Could be 10 x 1000m with 2-3 min jog rest, and the 5 x 200m. |
| Sun.   | Long run in the morning—around 1 hr 30 min. |

The times for the above intervals are of course individual, but though the effort should not be full speed, the athlete should finish the sessions tired out.

**Ismael Kirui,** World 5000m Champion of 1993 and 1995, sees little difference in his training for cross country and track running. "As long as the training is hard it does not matter too much what kind of training you do."

**Yobes Ondieki,** an athlete from Kisii District, has an outstanding range in distance running: 1500m—3:34.36, 1 mile—3:55.32, 2000m—5:01.6, 3000m—7:34.18, 5000m—13:01.82, 10,000m—26:58.38 and half-marathon—61:41! Ondieki, the first man in ten years to defeat Morocco's Saïd Aouita over 5000m, will perhaps be best remembered for his world record 10,000m and his world title 5000m in 1991.

His reputation among the Kenyans is that of a tough trainer. Patrick Sang and Richard Chelimo tell of such extremes as two track sessions per day. Ondieki never neglected pure speed in his training. A tough session for Yobes? "10 x 200m in 22-24 seconds with a short rest." And for the afternoon session? "10 x 800m at 10km race speed with 30 sec rest or less."

A believer in high altitude training, Yobes bases himself in Albuquerque, New Mexico (1600m). In the 1991 season in which Ondieki ran his personal best 5000m time, Yobes trained at home in Kenya and in Davos, Switzerland (1560m).

"I prepared well, but I didn't underestimate anyone. I knew I had to be ready for anything because I didn't know how well the others had prepared themselves." Running 13:01.82 in Zürich, Yobes realized he'd hit top form. Instead of his customary method of continuing hard training, Yobes backed off, reduced the work load and "took it easy." The result was a World Championship title in Tokyo.

**Daniel Komen** claims that intensity is the key word. He aims to make his training sessions harder and harder, believing there are no limits. Working off a two-minute jog recovery, Komen runs such workouts as 4 x 1 mile, the first run in 4:10 and the last close to 4:00. The training paid off last year, as Komen lopped an amazing four and a half seconds off Noureddine Morceli's "tough" 3000m record. Komen, who admitted to being "stunned" with the result, plans to attack the 5000m record next. His 12:45.09 in 1996 came close—it was the second fastest in history.

Komen lives up in the Kenyan highlands, outside the village of Kipkabus. The lush vegetation and red dirt roads make the area a runner's haven. "I am always running hills, they make me very strong."

**Barnabas Kitilit** earns his livelihood as a school teacher in the Eldama Ravine area, east of Eldoret. Kitilit is also an athletics coach and has advised and trained many of the leading runners in the area. Specializing in the 5000/10,000m, Kitilit produced the schedule below which he felt sure, if followed correctly, would elevate any male runner up to "Kenyan class."

Kitilit's latest success story is a runner named Simon Lopuyet who has been proving himself over the half and full marathon distance, including a win over a very classy field in the Lisbon Half-Marathon, backed up by an excellent debut fourth place in the 1995 New York Marathon. Kitilit demands dedication, sacrifice and the complete commitment of his runners. "The competition is so high these days that anything less just will not do—the runner will waste his time." A theme echoed among all Kenyan coaches.

| | AM 06.00 hrs | PM 16.00 hrs |
|---|---|---|
| Mon. | 8-12km. | 1km x 5 (run at 2:32-2:50), with 5 min rest or 800m x 5 (run at 1:56-2:00), with 5 min rest. |
| Tues. | 5-6km. | 8-10km. |
| Wed. | 5-10km. | 5km steady run. 10-12 x 400m (run at 60-68 sec), with one lap jog recovery. |
| Thurs. | 5-8km. | Hill work. |
| Fri. | 5-8km. | 10 x 200m (run at 24-30 sec), with 200m jog rest, or 10 x 300m (run at 39-46 sec), with 2 min rest. |
| Sat. | 5-8km. | Hill work. |
| Sun. | 5-8km optional. | Rest. However an evening session of 1-2 hrs running. |

"All runs must be fast enough and timed to note improvement," said Kitilit, who also stressed the importance of a good breakfast and a mid-morning rest.

# Lydia Cheromei

*"I just wake up and run as I feel."*

A schoolgirl star who was one of the first to prove that Kenyan women were potentially as talented as their male counterparts. Cheromei has had a relatively long career for a Kenyan female, beginning when she first burst onto the scene to win the World Junior Cross Country Championships at the age of thirteen, although Lydia herself admits that the age given was an estimate.

Despite medaling at the 1995 All-African games behind Rose Cheruiyot in the 5000m, championship track meets have not been rewarding for Cheromei. "I have no sprint. Usually I work so hard trying to tire everybody else out that I also am finished before the finishing line," explains Cheromei. However this work ethic did bring a junior world record of 14:53.44 for the 5000m in 1995, which stood as the Kenyan women's national record, as well.

**Lydia Cheromei**

Returning from Britain where Cheromei had been successful on the cross country circuit in 1996, Lydia was expected to "breeze" onto the Kenyan national team for the World Cross Country Championships. Cheromei, her boyfriend (and now husband) Hosea Kogo and their driver were heading for Eldoret for the Paul Kipkoech Memorial Cross Country race. Unfortunately their car crashed when a Kenyan taxi-bus *(matatu)* swerved to avoid a dead dog and they were blindsided by another *matatu*. Lydia received cuts and a slight concussion. The result was a three-week break and loss of form.

Lydia began "training" at an early age. "I had to run to school because I was usually late leaving the house. If I arrived late there would be a caning for me!" The 5km run four times a day, including the trip back and forth for lunch at home, provided Cheromei with the kind of daily mileage not many senior men get in—all this at the age of eight!

| | |
|---|---|
| Date of birth | Officially May 11, 1977. |
| Birthplace | Torongo, near Eldama Ravine. Tugen tribe. |
| Height/weight | 5-3¾ (162cm), 101-106 lbs (46-48kg). |
| Personal bests | 3000m—8:48.46, 5000m—14:53.44, 10,000m—31:41.09. |
| Honors won | World Junior Cross Country—1st (1991) and 3rd (1992) |
| | Kenyan national champion (1991 and 1992) |
| | All-African Games 5000m, 3rd (1995) and 10,000m, 2nd (1991) |
| | African Championships, 10,000m, 2nd (1992 and 1993) |
| | Kenyan and world junior record, 5000m (1995). |
| Home | Torongo. Teddington, England, over the summer and often St. Patrick's School for a training camp while in Kenya. |
| Coach | "Always have been self-coached. While in London I often run the group sessions set by Kim McDonald [her manager]." |
| Family | Married to Hosea Kogo, an international class Kenyan athlete. Lydia now calls herself Lydia Kogo. |
| Family runners | Two brothers, Jeremiah and Joseph Cheromei. Based in Italy the brothers compete, with some success, mainly in road races. The latter is a 2:10 marathoner. |
| Years running | Began running to school as a young girl around the age of eight. |
| Motivation | Run well in the Olympics. |
| Training sessions | Two per day. "I sometimes try three but often get too tired." |
| Tough session | Track work, 8 x 400m. |
| Training partners | Sonia O'Sullivan in London, with many Kenyans—Rose Cheruiyot, Florence Barsosio and the St. Patrick's students in the winter. "Anybody who is around!" |
| Favorite event | Cross country. "I am strongest running hills." |
| Kilometers per week | "Maybe around 90; usually 12-15km per day." |
| Comments | Lydia is another Kenyan who believes in putting in an honest effort. She trains usually from 25 minutes to one hour. "It is not worth putting on your track suit for less than 5km. How can you sweat hard in such a short time?" she questions. When in hard training Cheromei cuts out all distractions. |

"If you go around visiting, or strolling, then when the afternoon training session comes you are often tired and not able to put in a good effort."

Lydia likes to crotchet to relax. Running with others is important, she feels. "It is better to run with runners who can push you; always run a route where I have pushed with others so I can use my watch to remind myself of the pace I should be going." Cheromei feels though it is important to keep tabs on the work load. "The moment I train a lot I go out of shape. I have to keep under instead of doing too much." Lydia's race tactics are dictated by her lack of finishing speed. "I feel good pushing the pace; after half the distance I like to try and run from the field, but in the first half a good tactic for me is to be in the first two or three. If I get left behind by the lead group often I get dispirited and drop further and further down the field—my inspiration goes." Luckily for Lydia there are not too many competitors who can leave her behind!

## TRAINING PLAN FOR THE CROSS COUNTRY SEASON

Location: Iten. Altitude: 2300m. Surface: dirt road.

| Day 1 | AM | 45 min fast. | MID | 30 min fast. | PM | 6km fast. |
|---|---|---|---|---|---|---|
| Day 2 | AM | 35 min fast. | MID | "Too tired!" | PM | 8km varying pace. |
| Day 3 | AM | 35 min fast. | MID | 30 min steady. | PM | 7km fast. |
| Day 4 | AM | 30 min with hill work. | | | PM | 6km fast. |
| Day 5 | AM | 35 min fast. | | | PM | 6km planned; twisted ankle after 2.5km. |

Day 6   Rest.
Day 7   AM  40 min easy   MID  Travel to Nairobi.
Day 8   National Cross Country Championships. Dropped out after 4km

Lydia dislikes training on the track, though in the spring, mid-April, she begins to incorporate track sessions into her training, starting with two sessions per week and moving up to three. She competes from 3000m up to 10,000m and prefers the 5000m.

1 x 3000m—"Not often; the longest interval I have run!"
8 x 400m—short jog rest, "This one I do *not* like."
10 x 200m—"Not bad as they are over quickly."

2 x 800, 2 x 600 + 2 x 400m—"A usual session."
3 x 1000m—"A tough session, but better than the 400s."

"I like to run track sessions either in the morning or the afternoon, not at midday when the sun is at its hottest," says Cheromei.

Certainly there is nothing new or startling in Lydia's interval sessions. A difference may be that she likes to run good pace runs on the days between the interval sessions. "There is time for training and time for resting; the resting should not be mixed with the training." Lydia here repeats the typical Kenyan trait of making the training count. Kenyans believe the best form of resting is not easy running but staying at home relaxing! Track running does not come as naturally to Lydia as she would like, but as she has the second fastest 5000m among Kenyan women, she must be doing something right!

# Richard Chelimo

"Yes I used to be *very* tired in training!"

July 5, 1993, was a flawless evening for athletics, a sublime Scandinavian summer night. For Stockholm's DN Galan meet before a packed audience, Richard Chelimo had promised to attempt to set a 10,000m world record. The track in Stockholm had just six lanes in 1993 and the athlete felt the connection and the energy of the crowd just a few meters away. The Kenyan athletes who had competed earlier stood by the side of the track, in the athletes' enclosure, sensing something exceptional. "Man, that was one of the best races I have ever seen in my life!" remembers Patrick Sang. "We knew how hard he had been training."

Chelimo had prepared supremely for this race. The previous year Chelimo had lost, won, and again lost the Olympic 10,000m race in Barcelona. Owing to interference by a Moroccan runner during the final, Chelimo had been moved up to first place. A few hours prior to the medal presentation however, after a Moroccan protest, the decision was reversed. Chelimo raced around the streets of Barcelona trying to find a Kenyan official to lodge a further protest, but none were to be found. The gold was lost and a flame of injustice was fired within the soul of Chelimo—he *had* to run a race to confirm to the world who was the best 10,000m runner.

**Richard Chelimo during his 10,000 world record run in Stockholm.**

"I trained so hard for that race that the running of it was easy," said Chelimo. One of the more prominent names in the field was Arturo Barrios, a native Mexican who then held the world record for the event, 27:08.23. An Irishman, John Doherty, himself a world-class competitor, had been conscripted to pull the runners through the 5000m, and Chelimo then took over from Doherty. Using the runners he was about to lap as targets Chelimo pushed on, detached from the following pack. It was only after 7000m that the public realized a world record was feasible and they supported the Kenyan's efforts with a continuous deafening roar.

Chelimo broke the record by less than a second. He held it only for five days, however, before countryman Yobes Ondieki became the first athlete to dip below the 27-minute barrier. The memory for Chelimo nevertheless lives as bright as the gold medal he lost in Barcelona.

Chelimo has a house and a business in the running mecca of Kenya—Iten. The people of the town remember him more for an off-track incident than for his world record heroics. Late one night Chelimo parked the business's pickup truck outside his house. Just as he was locking the car door some machete-wielding robbers pounced upon him. Chelimo was forced to surrender both the automobile and the cash he was carrying. As the thieves made their getaway, Chelimo, dressed in his business suit, gave pursuit on foot. Townsfolk recollect the flash of light as Chelimo shot by, most swearing they had never seen a man run faster. A few moments after the vehicle had passed the regional police station—a couple of kilometers from Chelimo's home—Richard was in the same office registering an urgent complaint. The stolen car, cash and the criminals were soon captured and retrieved.

| | |
|---|---|
| Date of birth | April 24, 1973. |
| Birthplace | Kapyego, near Kapcherop. Marakwet district. |
| Personal bests | 3000m—7:41.63, 2 miles—8:26.29, 5000m—13:05.14, 10,000m—27:07.91. |
| Height/weight | 5-5 (165cm)/121 lbs (55kgs). |
| Honors won | 1992 Olympic 10,000m, 2nd |
| | 1993 World Record 10,000m |
| | 1991 World Championships 10,000m, 2nd |
| | 1993 World Championships 10,000m, 3rd |
| | World junior records, 5000 and 10,000m, 1990 |
| | 1990 World Junior 10,000m champion |
| | 1990 World Junior Cross Country, 2nd |
| | African 10,000m record, 1991 |
| | Commonwealth 10,000m record, 1991 |
| Home | House and farm in Kapcherop. House and general |

|                   |                                                                                                                                                                                                 |
|-------------------|-------------------------------------------------------------------------------------------------------------------------------------------------------------------------------------------------|
|                   | store in Iten and an apartment in Nairobi. Used to be based in London during the competition season.                                                                                            |
| Family runners    | Brother Ismael Kirui is two-time World Champion over 5000m. Sister Catherine Kirui has run some outstanding cross country races, finishing sixth twice in the World Junior Cross Country Championships. Moses Kiptanui, 3-time World Steeplechase Champion and record holder, is a cousin! |
| Years running     | Began running to school.                                                                                                                                                                         |
| Motivation        | "I just loved to run; it was born in me."                                                                                                                                                        |
| Occupation        | Businessman with a finger in many pies. Retired from the Army.                                                                                                                                   |
| Training sessions | Three per day, often two running and one of light exercises.                                                                                                                                    |
| Kilometers per week | In hard training often over 250.                                                                                                                                                               |
| Comments          | "Never run more than one hard session a day, otherwise you will 'kill' yourself... Don't overtrain once you have hit good form; just keep the body ticking with some light intervals," advises Chelimo. "You must not think about what training lies in front—just get it done... Never train alone with speedwork or you will never make it to your best ability... Training must come first, you cannot go to the city in the daytime and stroll around—training must be the main object of every day... Three months of hard training is enough; after that easy intervals to keep in shape for the races is what I do when in Europe." |

## TRAINING SAMPLES

One of Chelimo's favorite training sessions for the buildup stage is also one of the hardest to complete—for mere mortals. The track where Richard usually ran this session is a 400m dirt track complete with ruts and tufts of grass sprouting in the lanes! Add 2400m altitude and one soon begins to realize why Chelimo became the phenomenal runner he did. Although 15 min of jogging is shown below between the sets, this amount was rarely taken. Richard explains, "Often I would train in a group, but not many wanted to run this session. As we all traveled to the track in a pickup truck they would tell me to hurry the session up so we could leave. I usually cut the jog down to 5 minutes."

4 x 800m, to be run at 2:03-2:06, 80m jog rest between each 800m.

Jogging 15 min.

6 x 600m, to be run at 1:36, 80m jog between each 600m.

Jogging 15 min.

12 x 400m, to be run at 62 sec, 80m jog between each 400m.

"If you start the 400s and are hitting 58 seconds with ease then cut the session to 8 x 400m. You are now ready to run well, but it is not good to start with 58 seconds if you feel you cannot complete the session. Better to run 62s," explains Chelimo.

| | |
|---|---|
| Day 1 | 5 x 1000m, run at 2:35-2:37. 2 min jog rest + 1 x 400m in 58 sec. Another session of easy running, 30-40 min. |
| Day 2 | 70 min easy running. |
| Day 3 | 60 min normal speed. |
| Day 4 | 20 x 200m run at 29-30 sec, short rest. Another session of easy jogging. |
| Day 5 | 60 min normal speed. |
| Day 6 | 4 x 1600m run at 4:18-20, 200m intervals run at 28 sec between each of the mile repeats, jog rest. |
| Day 7 | Rest day. |
| Day 8 | 70 min normal speed. |
| Day 9 | 60 min + 40 min normal speed. |
| Day 10 | 60 min easy in the morning and rest in the afternoon. |
| Day 11 | 3000m competition, run between 7:57 and 8:00. |
| Day 12 | 60 min easy running. |
| Day 13 | 4 x 400m, 57-58 sec + 4 x 200m, 27-28 sec. 1½ min rest after each interval. Another session of easy running. |
| Day 14 | Rest. |
| Day 15 | 60 min easy jogging. |
| Day 16 | 30-40 min easy in the morning, and in the evening "now I am ready to run a 27 min 10,000m race." |

Another favorite track session of Richard's in the middle of a track season was to run 3 x 1200m, running each of the intervals at around 3:03, with a 2 min rest after each interval.

In the winter Chelimo is a great believer in the Armed Forces type of cross country training where the emphasis is on tempo runs. Running with a group of talented runners, Chelimo would push his body to exhaustion and beyond over the fast and fierce long tempo runs. The fartlek session is a grueling example of Chelimo's tough regime. "First, I would run for an hour at a good speed to tire the body out; then I would turn and run one hour's fartlek efforts all the way home." Chelimo always sought out the hardest sessions his body could manage. He knew that training was the key to running at world record speeds. Having family members to train with such as World 5000m Champion Ismael Kirui helped keep him on his toes.

Chelimo's strength was being able to push a strong pace, surge for a few laps and recover at the racing pace of the mortals in the race. In the hot and humid Tokyo 10,000m in 1991, Chelimo set out with a two-mile split of 8:34. Halfway was reached in a world class 13:30. Only Moses Tanui could hang on to such a pace!

Today, like other successful Kenyans, Chelimo is free with time and money to help young runners, and there are many who have benefited from his generous hand.

Will the great arenas see a comeback from Chelimo? It is highly possible. Chelimo is still a young man. If he ever decides to hire a business manager and go back into his hard training routine, then the world will undoubtedly see one of the greatest runners back to his winning ways. "I am thinking of joining the Armed Forces camp for a while to see what I can do!" Chelimo says, the faraway look in his eyes taking him from the town of Iten to the cheers of the adoring crowds screaming his name, willing him on and celebrating his sublime performances.

# The Marathon

| National Record: | Sammy Lelei 2:07:02, 1996 (2nd all-time) |
| | Tegla Loroupe 2:22:07, 1997 |
| Half-Marathon NR: | Moses Tanui 59:47, 1993 |
| | Tegla Loroupe 67:12, 1994 |
| Olympic Medals: | Silver—Douglas Wakiihuri 1988; bronze—Eric Wainaina 1996 |
| World Champs. Medals: | Gold—Douglas Wakiihuri 1987. |

*Since 1991 Kenyan men have won every Boston Marathon. In the 1996 race there were seven Kenyans in the top eight positions!*

Kenya has had less success in the marathon at the Olympics and World Championships than it has had in distance events on the track. The reason can be traced to economics. When you are an African marathoner, money has to be a main consideration.

"If you over-race you won't last at the top," explains Cosmas Ndeti. The race must pay if athletics is your career. Major sponsorships do not exist for Kenyan runners. If a Western athlete were to win the Olympic marathon, the sponsorship money would be substantial, but a Kenyan would probably receive nothing apart from a bonus from his shoe sponsor—if he had a bonus clause in his contract.

Competing in a major city marathon, a top runner—regardless of origin—can command an appearance fee, earn prize money and shoe company bonus money. "Boston was my jackpot!" laughed Moses Tanui, after collecting $100,000 in April 1996. Add to that figure appearance money and the bonus received from Fila sportswear and it totals a tidy amount.

There are no Olympic training grants in Kenya and there is no appearance money for the Olympics or World Championships. Since it is exceedingly difficult to run more than two world-class marathons a year, the top runner must choose his races with his finances in mind. All of the members of the Moi Air Base marathon squad admitted that winning Boston or New York is their dream achievement. The prize money at Boston is the same whatever country you come from; that is about the closest Kenyan athletes get to equality.

Despite the major championship "shortfall," Kenya has still accumulated three Olympic and World Championships medals in the marathon in the last nine years, a record superior to many "running" nations. The first came quite unexpectedly from **Douglas Wakiihuri,** a virtually unknown Kenyan who lived in Japan. The Kikuyu tribesman, born at sea level on the Kenyan East Coast, had gone to Japan in 1983 to train with Kiyoshi Nakamura, the famous coach who had brought Toshiko Seko into the marathon limelight.

Douglas Wakiihuri

Wakiihuri debuted in 1986 with a 2:16 and progressed the next year to 2:13, hardly harbingers of a gold medal at the World Championships in Rome. In that race he dueled with Ahmed Salah, then the second-fastest marathoner in history, striding away eventually to win the top place on the podium.

As an Olympic favorite in Seoul in 1988, he again battled with Salah, but this time there was a stronger runner—Gelindo Bordin of Italy (the third place finisher in Rome). Wakiihuri had to be content with the Olympic silver medal.

Sixteen months later he won the Commonwealth Games marathon in Auckland in 2:10:27. Then, after an absence on the world stage, Wakiihuri made a golden comeback in 1995, winning the Marathon World Cup in Athens.

Wakiihuri in training ran many long well-paced tempo runs between one hour and two. He would also train sprinting diagonally across a football field, jogging the straights. This type of session would typically last longer than one hour. Long runs were *long!*

Atlanta, with its heat and humidity, promised to be a challenge for the 1996 Olympic marathoners. After 20 miles, two runners pulled away from the pack: Josia Thugwane of South Africa and South Korea's Lee Bong-ju. Back in the pack, it was decision time—but only one runner set off to reel them in. **Eric Wainaina,** in the colors of Kenya, realized it was the break for the medals. Soon he made it a threesome at the front. The trio jockeyed back and forth. One would drop, then catch back up, then another would do the same. Few spectators hazarded a guess as to the eventual order of finish. The South African proved to be the strongest at the end and Kenya collected its first bronze Olympic marathon medal.

Kenyans have been labeled the free spirits of running. They run with their hearts, not their heads, some observers claim. It is true that it is not uncommon to see a Kenyan marathoner set off at breakneck speed, only to drop out or start walking later on. The self-belief the Kenyans have in themselves is unmatched, however, and their enthusiasm is understandable. Wilson Kiptum, a little-known runner training in Kapsabet, said, "I heard that [Sammy] Lelei ran very well in Berlin [2:07:02, the second-fastest marathon ever]. I know I can run faster than Lelei; if somebody takes me to a race with Lelei running, he will not beat me. I'll stick with him until the end; I don't care what pace he runs." This from a runner who has yet to beat 31 minutes for 10,000m!

Dieter Hogan, Uta Pippig's coach, advises some of Kenya's best marathoners. Michael Kapkiai is one of them. His 2:10:08 in the Turin Marathon was the 7th fastest time of 1994. "Hogan's ideas are very different from how I was running before, but they work for me. I think Sammy Lelei can thank Hogan [who coaches Lelei, also] for his 2:07 in Berlin."

# *A Week Of Michael Kapkiai's*
# *Marathon Training*

| | | | | | |
|---|---|---|---|---|---|
| Mon. | AM | 20km easy. | | PM | 5km medium. |
| Tues. | AM | 7 x 1600m, with 60 sec rest, @ 4:40. | | PM | 8km medium. |

| Wed. | AM | 35-40km at 4:30/km pace. | PM | Rest. |
| Thurs. | AM | 10km, 32 min. | PM | 15km easy. |
| Fri. | AM | Fartlek, 15km, session to be completed under 46 min. |
| Sat. | AM | 3-4 hrs very easy, run at 5 min per km. |
| Sun. | AM | 8km easy. | PM | Rest. |

"The emphasis is on being able to cover distance, then in separate sessions working on speed. In Kenya usually we just run everything at the fastest pace we can. The long run [on Saturday] is taken very, very easy. I think once Kenyans start following schedules, then more marathons will be totally dominated by our runners," says Kapkiai.

**Michael Kapkiai, left, with Peter Rono and Nixon Kiprotich, at Eldoret's Kipchoge Stadium. Photo by the author.**

# Armed Forces Marathon Training

Many of Kenya's top athletes are affiliated with the Armed Forces and train with other runners at the camp to achieve remarkable results—for instance, Jackson Kipngok's 2:08:08 in 1994. Athletes not in the service can also join the camp runners for training. William Musyoki, who resides a few kilometers from the N'gong faction, frequently links up with the military for marathon training. The group ordinarily will have no fewer than 15 fit full-time athletes. At the Laikipia Air Base there were around 40 marathoners in the fall of 1996, thus the training sessions were always competitive and never taken easy. The strong get stronger and the weak wilt!

Each morning of the training week below, a 40-70 min run is taken on a "how you feel" basis (about 06:00 hrs).

| Mon. | MID | 35-40km long run. | PM | Exercises and strolling. |
|---|---|---|---|---|
| Tues. | MID | Intervals, 5 x 1000m, 2 min rest. | PM | Jog 40-60 min, or strolling. |
| Wed. | MID | 90 min steady (after 30 min—full speed). | PM | Jog 40-60 min. |
| Thurs. | MID | Hills, 2 x 27 min continuous uphill running. | PM | Jog, plus exercises or rest. |
| Fri. | MID | Same as Wed. MID. | PM | "How you feel." |
| Sat. | MID | Tempo/fartlek run, full speed, 15km. | PM | Rest. |
| Sun. | | Day of rest, for the majority. | | |

**Eric Kimaiyo** is a typical Kenyan marathon success story. Living away from the city up in the Cherangani Hills, Kimaiyo trained primarily with long distance runs, some up to 50 kilometers, and most completed at a steady to good speed. No high-tech methods, no complicated training schedules. Each day was like the previous day—endurance running. This led Kimaiyo to a 2:10 marathon. "I just decided that I would try to become a runner, so I ran. It was that simple," laughed Kimaiyo, discussing his scientific approach to training.

**Benson Masya** is widely known for his prowess on the roads. With a personal best of 60:02 for the half-marathon and 2:12 for the full distance, Benson's trademark is *winning*. Nearly all the major road races between 5km and 21km have witnessed the fleet heels of Benson Masya.

Asked why he did not defend his world half-marathon title in 1993, Masya pointed out the economic disadvantage—the withdrawal of prize money.

Based in Southport, England, Masya differs in location but not in work ethic from other Kenyan distance stars. Training sessions for the marathon could be as extreme as two sessions of two hours distance running in the same day. Long strolls are also a hallmark of his schedule, a typical Kenyan activity.

"Fast distance runs develop the body best for road racing," says the three-time Honolulu Marathon champion (and ex-bantamweight boxer). "Most of the speed I have is from tempo runs, not intervals," explained Masya, when questioned about his ability to win races with powerful surges in the last few hundred meters. Friend Zablon Miano says, "Training with Benson is harder than competing. When he decides to run fast in the middle of a training run, *nobody* can run with him!"

**Sammy Lelei,** who in running the 1995 Berlin Marathon in 2:07:02 broke the Kenyan national record, lives a few kilometers outside Eldoret. "In Kenya I am never number one, but that is not important. Racing the shorter distances on Kenyan soil is tough preparation. They are part of the training," remarked Lelei, after finishing in a fairly high position in the Paul Kipkoech Memorial cross country race in Eldoret in January 1996.

Between Iten and Eldoret lies a large steep hill called Sergoit. "Whenever I was training in this area I always saw Lelei; he was running up and down this hill continuously, without rest." said neighbor William Koila. The diminutive (5 ft. 3 in./160cm) Lelei is an advocate of quantity. "I train lots!" When pushed for a figure, Lelei estimated around 150 miles per week in his marathon endurance phase.

JACK MCMANUS/PHOTO RUN

**Sammy Lelei**

Even as a spectator at a cross country competition, Lelei, dressed in a track suit, darted like a jackrabbit from viewing point to viewing point. Lelei joked that he took every opportunity to add up the miles!

Lelei's base is cross country. Back in 1992, he competed for the national team, but after draining himself with Mike Kosgei's camp schedule, he finished a lowly 77th at the World Championships. "I trained too much speedwork for too long a period." Previous to the camp Lelei had finished 9th in the

Kenyan nationals—a result at least equal to a top twelve World Championships position.

# Moses Tanui

Moses Tanui is a *distance* runner. We have become used to specialization in the athletics world—athletes concentrating on a single event, like Patrick Sang in the steeplechase and Cosmas Ndeti in the marathon. Tanui, however, challenges everything the distance program has to offer. Contemplate this résumé: two silver medals at the World Cross Country Championships; a gold and silver medal in the World Track & Field Championships at 10,000 meters—the silver won with a 56-second last lap, one shoe on, one off; a world-best time in the half-marathon and winner of the 1995 World Half-Marathon Championship; and winner of the prestigious 100th Boston Marathon (1996). Success on every surface.

In addition to running his own career, he coaches and assists several athletes back home in Eldoret. Two days before the 1996 IAAF Cross Country Challenge in Nairobi, Tanui was organizing how the junior runners from Rift Valley Province would make the trip to Nairobi. Tanui has this perspective on the matter: "When you are brought up in an extended family, you think wider, and helping

Tanui, one shoe on, one off, at the 1993 World Championships.

others is part of the process. They are like your sisters and brothers."

Tanui joined the international elite in 1988, with a sixth place finish at the World Cross Country Championships and an eighth in the Olympic 10,000m final. In the early 90s, he pretty much made the half-marathon distance his personal possession, winning the Stramilano Half-Marathon four times in a row. Two weeks after winning his second victory at the Great North half-marathon in Britain in 1995, he won the world crown at the distance.

Tanui's marathon debut came in 1993. He finished tenth that year at New York with a time of 2:15:36. Five months later he also came in tenth at Boston, but this time with a 2:09:40 clocking. At Boston the following year, he ran 2:10:22, but this time finished second to countryman Cosmas Ndeti.

The 100th Boston Marathon in 1996 was a major target for Tanui. "This time I tried and trained for Boston. . . I changed completely, running longer distances [in training]. Some people said I was just a 10,000m runner, but I knew with the right training I could run a good marathon."

He did, and he won in 2:09:16, his fastest-ever marathon. Some say, given the less favorable wind, that Tanui's time was the equivalent of Ndeti's 2:07:15 on the same course two years before.

| | |
|---|---|
| Date of birth | August 20, 1965. |
| Birthplace | Sugoi, 20km from Eldoret. Nandi tribesman. |
| Personal bests | 1500m—3:41.8, 2000m—5:03.7, 3000m—7:39.63, 5000m—13:17.80, 10,000m—27:18.32, half-marathon—59:47, marathon—2:09:16. |
| Honors won | World Championships 10,000m, 1991, 1st; 1993, 2nd |
| | 1995 World Half-Marathon Champion |
| | World Cross Country Championships 1990, 1991—2nd (4th in 1993) |
| | 1990 Commonwealth Games 10,000m, 2nd |
| | 1989 African Championships 5000m, 3rd; 10,000m, 2nd |
| | Boston Marathon 1995, 2nd; 1996, 1st. |
| Height/weight | 5-7 1/4 (171cm), 123 lbs (56kg). |
| Home | Eldoret. A farm at Sugoi. Based in Brescia, Italy, when training in Europe. |
| Coach | Self-coached, with advice from Dr. Gabriele Rosa of Fila Club. |
| Affiliation | K-Way team's first signing (later became the Fila team). |

| | |
|---|---|
| Family | Wife Leah. Three children—Kiprotich, Kiptoo and Miriam. |
| Years running | Training seriously since 1986. |
| Occupation | Retired army sergeant. Professional athlete. Budding rally driver. Tanui owns a race-prepared rally car. "If I find a good navigator I may consider driving the Safari Rally in the future." |
| Motivation | "To be world champion at four different events." He is halfway to achieving that goal. |
| Training sessions | Usually two per day. |
| Hard session | Hill run, gravel road 22km, starting at 1300m altitude, finishing at 2700m. 1 hr 30 min. |
| Kilometers per week | 200-240 in half-marathon training. 210-250 in marathon training. |
| Comments | "Know your own weaknesses." By trying the marathon distance, Moses knew that he had to work on his strength in the final 5km. Anyone who witnessed the final 5km at Boston in 1996 could see he had done his homework! "Run races at your own pace. . . When training for a big race don't disrupt the training with other races." Moses's philosophy on the marathon buildup is also somewhat different. He believes in just a month buildup. Of course, the runner will have trained normally prior to this month, but not at marathon intensity and volume. During cross country season Tanui always races and trains for that surface, believing that the strength gained there will hold him in good stead for the roads. "Good tactics in the marathon are to hang to the back of the lead pack for the first 20km so you keep out of trouble and have no problems at the water stations. In the second half you must be in touch because somebody can make a break to the finish." |

In April of 1996 the Kenyan Amateur Athletic Assocation held a track meet at Eldoret's Kipchoge Keino Stadium. Deplorably, the organizers forgot, or had not intended, to purchase prizes for the many participating athletes. Tanui, who was present as a spectator, directly drove into town and personally purchased prizes for the athletes—just one example of his generosity and assistance to the young athletes of his nation.

# TRAINING SAMPLES

February/March 1996, a month before Boston.

| | |  |  |
|---|---|---|---|
| Feb. 21 | AM | 70 min. | PM 60 min. |
| Feb. 22 | AM | 110 min. | |
| Feb. 23 | AM | 70 min. | PM 60 min. |
| Feb. 24 | AM | 25 min warm-up, 10 x 1km, 2 min recovery. | PM 60 min. |
| Feb. 25 | AM | Hill session, 22km uphill. | |
| Feb. 26 | AM | 70 min. | PM 60 min. |
| Feb. 27 | AM | 120 min. | |
| Feb. 28 | AM | 30 min warm-up, 20 x 1 min fast, 1 min slow. | PM 60 min. |
| Feb. 29 | AM | 60 min. | PM 60 min. |
| Mar. 1 | AM | 30 min warm-up, 4 x 3km, 3 min recovery. | PM 60 min. |
| Mar. 2 | AM | 60 min. | PM 60 min. |
| Mar. 3 | AM | 38km run in 2:15. | |
| Mar. 4 | AM | 70 min. | PM 50 min. |
| Mar. 5 | AM | 25 min warm-up, 25 x 1 min fast, 1 min slow. | |
| Mar. 6 | AM | Hill work, 22km in 1:28. | |
| Mar. 7 | AM | 70 min. | PM 70 min. |
| Mar. 8 | AM | 25 min warm-up, 4 x 3km, 3 min recovery. | PM 60 min. |
| Mar. 9 | AM | 70 min. | PM 60 min. |
| Mar. 10 | AM | 38km run in 2:15. | |
| Mar. 11 | AM | 60 min. | PM 50 min. |
| Mar. 12 | AM | 25 min warm-up, 12 x 1km, 2 min recovery. | PM 50 min. |
| Mar. 13 | AM | 70 min. | PM 60 min. |
| Mar. 14 | AM | Half-marathon. Fast. | |
| Mar. 15 | AM | 60 min. | PM 60 min. |
| Mar. 16 | AM | 30km run in 2 hrs. | |
| Mar. 17 | AM | 70 min. | PM 50 min. |
| Mar. 18 | AM | 25 min warm-up, 6 x 2km, 2 min recovery. | |
| Mar. 19 | AM | 70 min. | PM 60 min. |
| Mar. 20 | AM | 100 min. | |
| Mar. 21 | AM | 70 min. | PM 60 min. |
| Mar. 22 | AM | 25 min warm-up, 5 x 3km, 2 min. recovery. | PM 50 min. |
| Mar. 23 | AM | 70 min. | PM 60 min. |
| Mar. 24 | AM | 38km run in 2:15. | |
| Mar. 25 | AM | 70 min. | |
| Mar. 26 | AM | 25 min warm-up, 25 x 1 min fast, 1 min slow. | PM 60 min. |

When the schedule calls for two runs of about one hour per day, Tanui would run medium pace for one, easy for the other. The training surface was dirt roads and the altitude around 2000m.

This marathon schedule works! Four runners out of the top eight places in the 1996 Boston Marathon followed this schedule. The slowest of the four recorded 2:10:49.

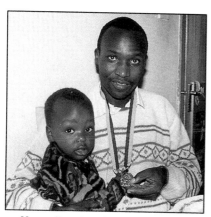

**Moses Tanui and son display the Boston Marathon medal. Photo by the author.**

For half-marathon training, Tanui believes in some slight modifications—reducing the mileage a bit and more emphasis on speed work. For adaptation, therefore, the structure would remain the same, the long runs shortened and the speed sessions run at increased pace.

"The important training is my hill session; this builds up my strength. In the training period I run this session twice a week, but if I have a competition then I run the hill just once." His hill training is legendary among the athletes of the Eldoret region. As you have seen, the hill is long—22km! And it starts at 1300m and gains another 1400m of altitude before the end! "I run this alone mostly; my driver drops me at the start and picks me up at the finish." Tanui takes a little under an hour and a half to complete the climb. "Yes, it is hard, but very good training; after running here you fear no hill!"

Before his victorious run at Boston, Moses took the last week easy. The last long run had taken place two weeks earlier.

| | |
|---|---|
| Mon. | 60 min steady. |
| Tues. | 50 min easy, extra stretching. |
| Wed. | 50 min of jogging, extra stretching. |
| Thurs. | 40 min of light running and stretching. |
| Fri. | 50 min of easy jogging, stretching. |
| Sat. | 40 min of easy jogging, stretching. |
| Sun. | Complete rest. |
| Mon. | Boston Marathon, 1st in 2:09:16. |

After finishing the race he rested one week before resuming training for the Olympic 10,000m. Lamentably, a leg injury forced him to drop out of the Kenyan trials after 15 laps. "I had been nursing a tendon ligament injury since Boston. The blistering pace worsened it. I won't take part in any race this summer," said Tanui.

Lately, Moses has been busy organizing races in Kenya, such as the Eldoret 10km in October 1996.

# *Tegla Loroupe*

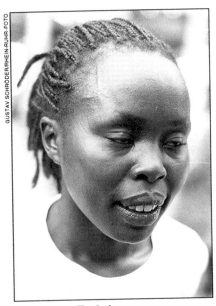

GUSTAV SCHRODER/RHEIN-RUHR-FOTO

**Tegla Loroupe**

Spearheading the Kenyan women's challenge in distance running is Tegla Chepkite Loroupe. The diminutive Kenyan's winsome smile and dancing eyes have made her a darling of the press and public, and her commitment and steel-hard training has brought her success on road and track.

Tegla made an immense impact on marathon running in her first try at the event, winning the 1994 New York Marathon. She had been concentrating pretty much on the 10,000m and cross country prior to 1994, and her win at New York started her on a new, profitable career.

In 1995, Loroupe returned to contest New York again. The week before her departure for the States, Tegla received the sorrowful news that her sister Albina had died due to a stomach hemorrhage back in Kenya. Tegla stopped training and yearned to return directly home to her family. In accordance with her sister's wishes, however, she reluctantly competed at New York. "When I was running, I could see her still smiling, looking happy."

Crossing the finish line first, Tegla burst into tears, releasing the emotions that had welled up inside her the entire previous week. It was an amazing performance—a 2:28:06 clocking on a very windy day. One of Tegla's victim was world champion

Manuela Machado of Portugal, who finished two and a half minutes behind.

The warm weather in August at Gothenburg (site of Machado's World Championships victory) would certainly have suited Tegla better than the cold and wind of New York, but Tegla opted for New York (in November)—a city she loves. She has won other road races there. "Coming to New York is like going home; I have so many lovely friends over there," recalled Tegla at her European base in Germany.

Three straight New York triumphs were not to be. Tegla started the 1996 race "all guns blazing." Unfortunately she ran out of ammunition and Tegla, who admitted to misjudging the pace, faded badly, finishing in 7th place.

| | |
|---|---|
| Date of birth | Listed date is May 9, 1973. |
| Birthplace | Kapsait, West Pokot District. |
| Height/weight | 5-$^1$/$_4$ (153cm), 88 lbs (40 kg). |
| Personal bests | 1500m—4:29.39, 3000m—9:04.42, 5000m—15:08.03, 10,000m—31:17.66, 15km—48:30, 10 miles—52:17, half-marathon—67:12, marathon—2:27:37. |
| Honors won | New York Marathon champion, 1994, 95<br>1996 Olympic 10,000m, 6th<br>World Championships 10,000m: 1993, 4th; 1995, 3rd<br>1993 World Half-Marathon, 3rd<br>Kenyan 10,000m record, 1993<br>Kenyan marathon record, 1994<br>1994 Goodwill Games 10,000m, 1st. |
| Home | Kapsait. A house also in Nairobi. Based in Detmold, Germany in the summer competition season. |
| Family | Single. "I'm concentrating on my athletics career." |
| Sponsor | Nike. |
| Coach | Volker Wagner. |
| Years running | Many years, ever since running to school—6-8km each way. Five years in Europe. |
| Reason for beginning | To earn a living and improve her future. |
| Occupation | Kenyan Post and Telecommunications Corporation representative. |
| Training sessions | Two per day. |
| Favorite session | "Speedwork of all kinds." |
| Tough session | "Speedwork!" |
| Hardest session | 30 x 400m run in 78 sec. |
| Motivation | To break the marathon world record in 1997-98. |
| Best achievement | Lisbon half-marathon in 1996. |
| Family runners | A sister who is beginning. No others in the immediate family. |

Kilometers per week  160-170.

Comments                  Tegla, like the majority of Kenyans, sees the posi-
                          tive side of training with others. While staying in
                          Germany she lives with a group of Kenyan ath-
                          letes, many from her home district. Before New
                          York in 1996, she trained with Joyce Chepchumba,
                          who was to finish 3rd in New York and earlier in
                          the year was runner-up in the London Marathon.
                          "Sometimes it is good to run alone also, to gather
                          your thoughts." Training is monitored by how the
                          body feels. If the muscles are tired and achy, then
                          Tegla can run two easy sessions of 45 min to re-
                          cover. If she feels strong, however, then the morn-
                          ing session is a quality workout with again 45 min
                          of easy running in the evening.

                          The philosophy behind Tegla's marathon
                          buildup is one of preparation through both qual-
                          ity and quantity. The long run, once a week, is two
                          and a half hours in length. Intervals, often twice a
                          week, are tough—for example, 3 x 3km at mara-
                          thon pace with two min jog recovery. 15 x 1km at
                          faster than race pace, 3:18 per km, is another typi-
                          cal session.

When asked about her training, she explained the difference
between 10,000m and marathon training is minimal. She just increases the length of her weekly long run for marathon training.
Tegla trains similarly to Rose Cheruiyot and Lydia Cheromei—a
lot of well-paced tempo runs. One of Tegla's individual traits,
however, is that she loves running a long hill session—a session
that could be 12km or more of steady uphill running.

Her cousin and training partner, Wilson Musto, says, "Tegla
is tough; she likes hard training. No resting for her." Jacob Losian,
who was born in Tegla's village and is one of the Kenyans who
lives and trains with her in Germany, reckons that daily life in
his village, Kapsait, is a tough breeding ground for success in
endurance running.

After completing a marathon Tegla takes a month's rest before resuming training. The marathon buildup takes on average
three months and Tegla likes to include some shorter races as
sharpeners. She also feels that she is still very competitive at
10,000m. "I do not want to run too many marathons too soon.
That is why I concentrated on the 10,000m at the Olympics; [it
was] too soon after Boston to run another marathon." (She had
finished second to Uta Pippig in that April race, winning $50,000.)

## A Typical Marathon Training Week

| | | | | |
|---|---|---|---|---|
| Mon. | AM | 60 min easy, 15km. | PM | 60 min easy, 15km. |
| Tues. | AM | 90 min normal speed. | | |
| Wed. | AM | 1-2 hrs easy. | PM | 60 min easy. |
| Thurs. | AM | Interval session. | PM | 90 min easy. |
| Fri. | AM | 75 min easy. | PM | Jogging. |
| Sat. | AM | 2½ hrs easy, long run. | | |
| Sun. | AM | 90 min easy, until the last 30 min (run hard). | | |

Tegla's light-on-her-feet running action is virtually perfect for marathon running. Normally starting off behind her major competitors, Loroupe ropes them in as the kilometers unfold, her effortless stride enduring against the fatigue that attacks all.

A Boston victory still eludes her. In her first Boston (1995) she was "overtired by running too many races." She suffered stomach pains and finished 9th in a respectable 2:33. In 1996 she nearly pulled off the win, but was swallowed up in the final miles by Uta Pippig.

Boston does remain one of Tegla's important goals. She promises to practice drinking on the run, as both her Boston Marathons have given her problems collecting her bottles from the drinks tables. "Lack of practice," she says. "In Kenya I am never drinking on my long run." Don't bet against the diminutive Kenyan in the next Hopkinton-to-Boston race.

## Cosmas Ndeti

Cosmas Ndeti was little known to the athletics world at the beginning of 1993.

In 1988, he finished second at the World Junior Cross Country Championships in Auckland, but he tested positive for Piriton following the event. He had ingested it in a cold remedy. The team doctor was blamed for the foul-up and the IAAF gave Ndeti a minimal three-month ban, but denied him his silver medal.

He experienced some success two years later, winning the 20km road race at the 1990 World Junior Championships. He went to train in late 1991 in Japan with the Konica team, but he found the training unsuitable. "I got slower and slower; we ran huge distances every day." It was road ace and Ndeti's relative Benson Masya who advised Cosmas to concentrate on the marathon.

"Benson has always helped me. We have trained many times together. The Kambas [Ndeti's tribe] are not as famous as the Kalenjin for running, but we have a lot of world-class runners."

In December, 1992 Ndeti finished second (to Masya) in the Honolulu Marathon. This was to prove to be an important stepping stone. The Kenyans were sending a group to run the Boston Marathon in April and the last available place was offered to Ndeti because of his good Hawaii showing.

Jayne Ndeti, Cosmas's wife, remembers: "This was a big time in Ndeti's life. In March he was reborn and saved; after that his life took on new meaning." Prior to that turning point, Cosmas had been having problems. "Alcohol has ruined many athletes in this country," he says. "At one time I fell victim, until March 1993, when

**Cosmas Ndeti**

I sought Jesus Christ to be my saviour." A month later he won his first Boston Marathon in 2:09:33.

Even as reigning Boston champion, Ndeti wasn't considered a favorite to repeat in 1994. After all, he was just one of many Kenyans in the race, all with international credentials. And Ndeti had no results to speak of since the previous Boston.

The 1994 race turned out to be a tactical masterpiece with a fight to the finish. Ndeti won again, holding off Andres Espinosa of Mexico by a scant four seconds. The clock was stopped at 2:07:15, then the fifth fastest time ever—and a course and Kenyan record.

The quality of the field and the outstanding time validated Ndeti as one of the world's best marathoners.

Ndeti again disappeared from public view for another year. From April to August he rested. "I didn't run a step! I put on 16 pounds!" There was much speculation as the 1995 race approached. Could the Kenyan pull off a Boston hat trick? A 68-minute half-marathon time on one of the world's fastest courses a couple of months before Boston did nothing to encourage Ndeti's supporters.

But again, using his familiar tactic of sitting in the lead group before storming away in the final kilometers, Ndeti won by a minute, recording his third straight win (and another sub-2:10 mark).

## BOSTON SPLITS

| 1993 | 1st half: 65:12 | 2nd half: 64:21 | Overall: 2:09:33 |
| 1994 | 1st half: 65:00 | 2nd half: 62:15 | Overall: 2:07:15 |
| 1995 | 1st half: 64:52 | 2nd half: 64:30 | Overall: 2:09:22 |

The average is 2:08:43! "The first 16 miles are to be run carefully or the legs will be too tired for the last ten miles. Because of the downhill too many runners go too fast. The marathon is about waiting, then attacking."

A mediocre performance in the December 1995 Fukuoka Marathon seemed to bode well for Ndeti's chances at the 1996 Boston, if his 1995 experience was anything to go by. But Ndeti had suffered in the cold and irritated an old calf injury as he struggled to 24th place in Japan, though still with a respectable 2:15:40 time.

Still he publicly proclaimed that a world record time was possible in Boston and the media attention was intense. In addition to the record prediction, this was the historic 100th Boston Marathon and Ndeti was shooting for his fourth victory in succession.

Ndeti started fast, uncharacteristically so, leading a collection of world-class Kenyans—all aiming at that record Ndeti had forecast. A fourth win was not in the cards for Cosmas. Moses Tanui and Ezekiel Bitok ran superbly, shunting him to a still very respectable third position. His 2:09:51 mark gave him four straight Boston Marathon times under 2:10. The bronze medal was a great accomplishment but certainly a frustrating experience for a runner who had been used to making Boston his "celebration."

A popular man in the local community, Cosmas has not forgotten his roots. Financial support for the building of a church, equipping church choirs, and paying school fees for poor children are some of the philanthropic ways Ndeti has used his newfound affluence. "It doesn't hurt to share the little you have with others," says Ndeti.

*"Your athletic ability and commitment to excellence are inspiring."*
From a letter to Ndeti from U.S. President Bill Clinton

| | |
|---|---|
| Date of birth | Listed as November 24, 1971. |
| Birthplace | Mua Hills, near Machakos. Kamba tribe. |
| Personal bests | 5000m—14:03.5, 10,000m—28:31.48, half-marathon—61:04, marathon—2:07:15. |
| Honors won | World Junior Championships 20km road race 1990, 1st |
| | Kenyan national marathon record, 1994 |
| | Boston Marathon 3-time winner, 1993-94-95 |
| Height/weight | 5-10 (178cm), 137 lbs (62kg). |
| Home | Mua Hills. Trains often with Benson Masya in Southport, England. |
| Coach | Self-coached. "I know my own body best." |
| Family | Wife Jayne. Two children—Sarafina and Gideon Boston. Comes from a large family of 36 brothers and sisters. Not surprisingly, his father had more than one wife. |
| Years running | Began running to and from Chasita Primary School. Became interested in athletics at Kwangiise Secondary School. |
| Family runners | His mother's father was a runner. "It is me Cosmas gets his blood for running from," the proud grandfather reveals. Brother Josephat is an international standard athlete achieving success in the long distance events. |
| Motivation | "Ibrahim Hussein and Douglas Wakiihuri I saw were both winning races." |
| Occupation | Professional runner. Farm owner. |
| Training sessions | Two per day. |
| Kilometers per week | 180-200. |
| Hobby | A boxing fan, especially Mike Tyson. Cousin Benson Masya is a former bantamweight boxer. |
| Comments | "Run races with your head. Watch the other runners, then you can see when they are tired. Then you can attack." Cosmas feels it is important to stay focused about the main race you are planning for. "When I ran 68 [minutes] at the Lisbon Half [1995], everybody was saying that I could not win |

in Boston. However it was only a preparation race. Plus it was windy and I don't like running in the wind." What was important to the journalists mattered not to Ndeti. He knew where he was heading and when he planned to run fast. "God is my inspiration and has helped me through times of difficulty." Ndeti can come across as a brash character, full of self-belief and confidence. The real Ndeti, however, away from the cameras, is a sensitive and caring man.

## TRAINING PLAN

After running in Fukuoka in December 1995, Ndeti recuperated for three weeks. "I ate and rebuilt my strength. No running, no nothing." Ndeti drove around in his new white Subaru, giving his muscles a complete break. Training for Boston 1996 commenced on December 30.

One of Ndeti's greatest assets is his ability to concentrate on the training at hand. Cosmas's brother, Josephat, says, "When Ndeti is training he is very serious. His life is training for the race."

First Ndeti launched into the endurance phase, building up a foundation of durability. "If I feel like running fast, I do; if I feel like an easy session, then it is easy." This phase included several runs of roughly 21km, segments of which would be run on roads to simulate marathon conditions. "The tarmac helps prepare my legs for the hard surface in the race."

Regularly Cosmas would run high up into the Mua Hills to gain leg strength. In February he flew to Southport, England, to continue the endurance phase and to do some long tempo runs with fellow Kamba runners domiciled in England. Unfortunately the changeable weather did not help much.

Ndeti must be the only African elite athlete to consider moving his training from Kenya to England in the wintry month of February. Why? "The weather in Machakos is very hot. You have to run early in the morning, then again in the late afternoon. When I am in Southport I get up about 9 o'clock, eat some breakfast and drink tea, relax, then go training around 10 o'clock. That is how I like it. Usually, by that time, the weather is not so cold."

In March Ndeti chose to join the Kenyan national cross country team for training. He runs the same exact sessions as the other runners, but adds long runs. "This is my speedwork period. It suits me well, as they train very hard." In 1996, however, the cross country crew location changed from Embu, Mount Kenya, to N'gong. Ndeti decided not to disrupt his plans and remained at Mount Kenya for the last six weeks prior to flying to Boston the week before the marathon.

In the concluding six weeks, Ndeti also ran a time trial over a course that usually takes considerably more than two hours. After finishing the run in 2:09, Ndeti felt he was in form superior to the previous years he had run at Boston. "I am not only going for the fourth title, but my mind is focused on breaking the world record. I'll go for an early lead, let them follow me and I pray and believe that with God's guidance I'll realize my dreams." In the future perhaps; 1996 did not work out as he had hoped.

But don't count him out. "Yes, I am going to win again," says Ndeti, putting the marathon world on notice.

## NDETI'S TRAINING BLOCK FOR THE MARATHON

| | |
|---|---|
| **Rest Period** | Minimum of one month complete rest. Eat good foods. Gain weight. Intertwine both mental and physical restoration of the body. |
| **Endurance Phase** | Two sessions per day, morning and evening. The key session during this period is the 21km run, partially on tarmac. These runs typically are run at a fair clip. A long run once a week over 2 hrs. Runs up into the Mua Hills to build strength. Two months. |
| **Speed Phase** | An injection of high speed with intervals and fartlek. Tempo runs at a pace which makes marathon pace feel pedestrian. Training with athletes who are aiming at competing at 5-10,000m. Long runs, two hours. One month. |
| **Tapering Phase** | A timed tempo run at altitude of more than two hours. Run hard! The last week after traveling to the race site, just easy running, with sessions of 40 min. Two weeks. |

# Cross Country

***Kenya at the World Cross Country Championships (through 1997):***
*Senior men—10 individual winners (1986-89, 1992-97); 12 team win-*
*ners (1986-97)*
*Senior women—1 individual winner (1994); 5 team winners (1991-*
*93, 1995-97)*
*Junior men—9 individual winners (1985, 1987-88, 1990, 1992-94,*
*1996-1997); 10 consecutive team winners (1988-97)*
*Junior women—4 individual winners (1991, 1993-94, 1997); 8 team*
*winners (1989-91, 1993-97)*

*In the last eleven years, 34 out of 42 team titles have been won by the*
*Kenyan national team. In 1994, William Sigei, Helen Chepngeno, Phillip*
*Mosima and Sally Barsosio completed a grand slam, taking all the four*
*individual titles. In 1993 the Kenyan senior men took positions 1, 2, 3,*
*4, 5 + 10, using none of their top three finishers from the 1992 Champi-*
*onships!*

To say that the Kenyans have dominated world cross country running is something of an understatement. During the last
decade, beginning with the Mike Kosgei era, Kenyans have anni-
hilated the opposition with their depth of talent. With just three
individuals (Ngugi, Sigei and Tergat), the senior men have taken
ten individual titles in twelve years. Considering that the 1997
junior men's team won, scoring just thirteen points with positions 1, 3, 4, 5, and 6, the pattern is set to continue.

The World IAAF Cross Challenge is a race series to deter-
mine the best overall cross country runner for the whole season.
It was no surprise that the Kenyans took individual honors in
both the male and female classes in 1996.

What is the secret of Kenyan success? The answer lies in title
of this book—Train Hard, Win Easy. The Kenyans take cross country running seriously, equal in importance to track and field.
Kenyan runners fight tooth and nail for a place on the national
squad and believe that victory is secured before the race is even

run. "We will not let any team defeat ours; there is NO way," laughed Charles Kwambai on his way to the World Championships in South Africa. He was right!

**Ondoro Osoro** has been a prolific cross country runner for many years. In 1991 Osoro was the winner of the World IAAF Cross Challenge and runner-up the following year. The "secret" ingredient in Osoro's training was hard hill running, "I would run two times in the week up a long steep hill in Nakuru for about 12 kilometers." Ondoro did not take this session at an easy pace either. "Yes, I would be sweating hard after this one!" laughed Ondoro who has a 27:24 personal record for the 10,000m.

"Have you run in the mud yet?" questioned Simon Chemoiywo. "It is very good, builds up good strength, makes running in Europe much easier." When the rains fall on the red dirt roads, a glutinous "honey" surface is formed. The mud clings in clumps to your shoes, making them extremely heavy. The hip muscles strain to lift the limbs. Undoubtedly training under such conditions builds up incredible leg strength and mental mettle that truly makes the Kenyans believe that over smoother surfaces they will be unbeatable.

"It does not matter whether you run the 800m or the marathon, the cross country training is very important; it builds strength for all distances." tells Kip Cheruiyot.

**William Sigei** looked to emulate the great John Ngugi in the early 90s. In fact, it was a victory over Ngugi in a local 5000m race that catapulted Sigei's name to the forefront of Kenyan athletics. Sigei was thereupon recruited by the Kenyan Air Force team and his career took off. He twice won the Kenyan national cross country title (1993 and 1994) and the same years he won the World Championship title. On the track, Sigei will always be remembered for cutting over six seconds from Yobes Ondieki's year-old 10,000m world record in Oslo, 1994. At this writing, Sigei was building a new house on a piece of land he calls "Oslo," in the town of Bomet.

"My tactic was to start very fast and maintain the pace." The tactic worked; very few could match Sigei's speed endurance. Simeon Rono, a neighbor of Sigei's, remembers that Sigei would nearly always train alone. At the pace he churned out his miles it had to be that way! "Sigei trained *very* hard; when that man is motivated, he is the best runner in Kenya," adds Rono. Sigei's favorite session was the regulated fartlek advocated by Mike Kosgei—2 minutes hard with one minute easy over a 10km course. Even though the altitude exceeded 2000m and route was quite hilly, Sigei would run this session in about 31 minutes.

The Armed Forces use cross country training generally from November to March. Basically the schedule is carbon-copied week in, week out. The work is seen as foundation training for any type of running. A typical week:

| | | |
|---|---|---|
| Mon. | AM | 40-90 min "how you feel." |
| | MID | Long run, starting steady and finishing fast, 1 hr 30 min. |
| | PM | 40 min easy jogging. |
| Tues | AM | Same as Monday AM. |
| | MID | Fartlek, 1 hr. |
| | PM | Same as Monday PM. |
| Wed | AM | Same as MondayAM. |
| | MID | Tempo run, 70 min, extremely hard. |
| | PM | Same as Monday PM. |
| Thurs. | AM | Same as Monday AM. |
| | MID | Hill work, 27 min constant uphill. |
| | PM | Same as Monday PM. |
| Fri. | AM | Same as Monday AM. |
| | MID | Steady run, 70 min, commonly up to full speed after 20 min. |
| | PM | Same as Monday PM. |
| Sat. | AM | Same as Monday AM. |
| | MID | Tempo run, 60-80 min, flat out OR competition. |
| | PM | Rest. |
| Sun. | | Rest day. |

The training is rather similar to that of the marathon runners who often do cross country training before beginning their marathon buildup. Stephen Langat elucidates: "After my last marathon of the year, I rest for a few weeks; then I join the cross country runners for a couple of months. Three months before the first marathon of the year I change and begin marathon preparation." The main differences is the distances covered, the cross country runners tackling lesser mileage.

# John Ngugi

"To be a champion you must be prepared to train very hard."

One of the most famous names in Kenyan athletics is that of John Ngugi. When he first started, he was advised to go home and not waste his time training to become an athlete. Army coach Kiplimo explains. "When he walked his feet stuck out, and his style looked even worse when he ran. They sent him away from the training camp. Ngugi just trained harder. He returned later and showed them he could run. The rest is history."

Ngugi's lope captured an extraordinary string of five World Cross Country Championship titles, an Olympic gold medal and a Commonwealth Games silver.

At the World Championships in Rome (1987), Ngugi faded to 12th place in the 5000m final. A large cyst was found to be a problem and was removed after Rome. Going into the Olympics in Seoul the following year he was thought to be just another Kenyan, one who ran well in cross country.

**John Ngugi's great stride. He is shown here winning the 1992 World XC Championships in Boston.**

The Olympic 5000 final began at a dawdle, the first 800m going in 2:11. Ngugi pounced virtually from last place after the first kilometer and tossed in a 57.8 lap, a pace normally reserved for 1500m runners. He passed the field in one big move and kept pressing to open up a sizable gap. Ngugi hammered on never to be caught. It was a reckless way to run but it paid off with the gold medal. This is the kind of "mad" tactic that fires the public imagination about Kenyan runners. Years later, asked about his Seoul strategy, Ngugi commented, "I was afraid it would be down to a sprint finish and my kick is not that good—so I decided to make the race fast."

Ngugi will perhaps be remembered even more for his five cross country titles. Although tall in stature (compared to other Africans), Ngugi seemed to float effortlessly over any terrain and glide away from his competitors—more often than not opening huge winning margins. In the mud of Stavanger, Norway, Ngugi ran back in the pack until the orders came from Mike Kosgei. Then he shot ahead and surged to an insurmountable lead. To prove his versatility, Ngugi's last victory (1992) was won running in snow, not a surface the Kenyan had prepared for back home! The wintry conditions in Boston did not bother him as he romped to a 15-second victory over teammate William Mutwol.

| | |
|---|---|
| Date of birth | May 10, 1962. |
| Birthplace | Nyahururu. Kikuyu tribe. |
| Personal bests | 3000m—7:45.59, 5000m—13:11.14, 10,000m—27:11.62, half-marathon—61:24. |
| Honors won | World Cross Country champion 1986, 1987, 1988, 1989, 1992 |
| | 1988 Olympic 5000m champion |
| | 1990 Commonwealth Games 5000m, 2nd (fell) |
| | Kenyan national 5000m champion 1988 and 1989 |
| | 1987 All-African Games 5000m champion |
| | 1985 African Championships 5000m, 3rd |
| | Commonwealth 10,000m record, 1990 |
| Height/weight | 5-10 (178cm), 139 lbs (63kg). |
| Home | Nyahururu. Lives at Crystal Palace when in England. |
| Coach | Mike Kosgei and self-coached, plus advice from John Bicourt in recent years. A product of the Armed Forces training camp. Kosgei coached him before each of the cross country titles and before Seoul in 1988. "He made me what I am today. I, and a host of other top runners, owe it all to him," said Ngugi. |
| Family | Wife Alice and two sons, Steven and James. |

| | |
|---|---|
| Years running | "Many, many years before I won in 1986 (his first world title). . . I began, like many Kenyans, by running to school." |
| Family runners | Brother James Kamau Kariuki, second overall in the 1995/6 World Cross Challenge. |
| Motivation | To win a sixth World XC title. . . and conquer the marathon. |
| Inspiration | "Henry Rono was my hero." |
| Occupation | Senior Sergeant, Kenyan Army. General store owner in Nyahururu. |
| Training sessions | Used to be three daily, but now often two. |
| Kilometers per week | When in hard training, 1987-1992, above 240 |
| Comments | "Never give up; just work hard." Ngugi believes that the key to success is to build the body with training loads that would scare the average athlete."Back in 1990 we were training together and it was supposed to be an easy day, as we'd trained very hard the day before. Well, Ngugi decides to do a few kilometer repeats—he does twenty!" laughs Richard Chelimo, himself remembered as a formidable trainer. Ngugi often likes to run *that* bit farther than his training partners. Kosgei says, "Ngugi would get up an hour earlier than everybody else and run an extra ten kilometers."Ngugi believes in using low-key races as part of training. After finishing 108th (!) in a Kenya AAA cross country race, he smiled, "This is all part of the ongoing process of training. In Kenya I am always expected to win, but during hard training it is impossible." This reinforces Chelimo's point that when the buildup period takes place all else must be secondary, even competition. |

## TRAINING SAMPLE

Training for cross country. Kenya. Winter. The main day's session:

| | |
|---|---|
| Day 1 | 40-50 min easy. |
| Day 2 | Hill work, repeats up a steep 300m gradient. |
| Day 3 | 2 hrs, ending hard. |
| Day 4 | 10x1km, cross country, short rest. |
| Day 5 | 70 min steady. |
| Day 6 | Some form of hill work. |
| Day 7 | Fartlek or intervals (15x400m, short jog rest). |
| Day 8 | 70 min steady. |
| Day 9 | Cross country intervals (10x1km, short jog rest). |

| Day 10 | 1 hr steady. |
|--------|--------------|
| Day 11 | Hill work, 25x200m. |
| Day 12 | 1 hr, strong finish. |
| Day 13 | Long run, 90 min. |
| Day 14 | Fartlek over 15km. Hilly terrain. |

## TRACK TRAINING

Quality with quantity was Ngugi's successful recipe. Ngugi believed in maintaining a large work load in the summer buildup period, often combining heavy distance runs in the morning with hard track sessions later in the day. The day's key session:

- 20-30x400m run in 62-65 seconds, with 100m jog rest.
- 15-20x1000m run in 2:40-2:50, with 200m jog rest.
- 3x5000m, run under 15:00, 3 min jog recovery.
- 10x800m, run in 2 min, with an equal recovery. "This I would use to build speed."

Often the "warm-down" would become a tempo session. "If I felt strong then I would train hard, yes, hard!" He has no qualms about training hard the day prior to competition.

Typically Ngugi would run a session at 06.00 hrs, as with the majority of the Armed Forces team. He would cover 12-20km at a pace he would call "steady." Mere mortals would call the pace "fast." Try 1 hr 10 min for a 22km very hilly morning run as a warm-up for the day's main session! In the afternoon a stroll, light exercises or a slow run would be taken at 15.00 hrs or so.

Before each of the speed sessions a warm-up, consisting of jogging for 15 minutes and some light exercising and stretching, would be undertaken to "wake" the body. Ngugi has the ability to push his body harder and harder, even if he trains by himself.

Ngugi would often be a mere mortal himself before the training camps. Mike Kosgei remembers the period before the 1992 camp. "Let's just say Ngugi was not all that focused on running. However when I brought him away from the town and into the camp he focused totally on training." The result was another cross country title.

An unfortunate note to the Ngugi story is the misunderstanding over a drug test that cost him a suspension in 1993 from the athletics world. It was the first year the IAAF had initiated home visits to check athletes for possible doping violations. Deplorably, no one told Ngugi, who was accustomed to giving samples at stadiums or athletics centers.

Kenya is a poor country and opportunists abound. Ngugi has

to arrange for guards at his general store. Suspicion of strangers is natural, especially after the experiences Ngugi has had. When the IAAF official arrived, Ngugi's explanation is that he thought him to be a fan seeking a photo or a handshake. He completely misunderstood the whole situation, which resulted in the official having to leave empty-handed.

Ngugi committed an offense under the rules of the IAAF, technically equal to an admission of taking a banned substance. Despite a number of appeals from the Kenyan federation, reinstatement came only after more than two and a half years of the suspension were served. Ngugi's weight ballooned and his conditioning during the suspension was nonexistent. "Ah, to come back in Kenya is so hard. Ngugi can return to good form, but it would take years for him to build up his form again to the level he was when he was at his best, and Ngugi is an old man now," comments William Sigei. Whether he will ever return to the form which the world was fortunate enough to witness in the late 80s and early 90s is doubtful. But as Mike Kosgei says, "If one man is capable of coming back against the odds, it is Ngugi!"

# Paul Tergat

Paul Kibii Tergat has shown himself to be one of the most dynamic of Kenya's distance running corps over the past few years. A succession of fine road performances, scintillating track results and three World Cross Country titles demonstrate that Tergat is one of the world's elite.

After a leg injury curtailed training in 1992, Tergat rested the normal Kenyan way—he ate, relaxed and put on weight. Kenyans are not advocates of alternative exercise!

When the injury subsided, Tergat began to train hard again. He also dieted hard to drop the extra pounds he had added. The result? "I came down [in weight] too quickly. Sure, I could run well, but I did not have any strength. I used to finish training sessions close to fainting."

Back to normal, Tergat hit excellent form in 1995. In the World Cross Country Championships the strategic orders from Mike Kosgei were the only thing that held Tergat back. As soon as Kosgei gave the word, Tergat spurted ahead. He opened a 100-meter gap on his pursuers and ran untroubled to the finish.

In the following month, Tergat won the Stramilano Half-Marathon in 59:56, the year's best time and only the second official time ever recorded under one hour. His form continued over the summer and he collected a commendable bronze medal at the World Championships in Sweden in the 10,000m, stopping the clock at 27:14.70, a personal best.

The strategy discussions before the 1996 World Cross Country Championships centered on Haile Gebrselassie. Gebrselassie had won the 10,000 meters at the World Championships in 1995 and had demolished the world record in both the 5000 and 10,000m. His 1996 season had begun well, as he lopped ten seconds from the indoor 5000 record and five seconds from Kiptanui's indoor 3000 record. Even the newspapers in Kenya were expecting an Ethiopian victory.

Meanwhile, training in the N'gong hills was a man who knew only one thing—he who trains hardest wins. "If someone beats me, then I am happy for him; he will have obviously worked harder for the result than I did," says Tergat. For Paul, the season was also shaping up well, with a couple of cross country victories and a close loss to Moses Tanui, hardly a disgrace.

The National Championships were Tergat's first major test. "The important race of course is in South Africa. It is only important for me to run a good race here. My family do not have the chance to see me compete often, so here is a good opportunity." His family were there in force and they expected victory. Paul did not disappoint them. He ran with the lead pack until the planned breakaway point at 8km, then cantered home to win his third national title.

The following week was the IAAF cross challenge in Nairobi. Few foreigners bothered to come to this race. It is strenuous enough to try to run with Kenyans when they are on foreign

VICTOR SAILER/PHOTO RUN

**Paul Tergat**

soil, but on home ground and at altitude, it is a fruitless endeavor. The contest was one of the hardest cross challenges to win due to the fact that 60 of the best Kenyans were entered. But Tergat won easily—he was in great form. The attention of the Kenyan sportswriters turned away from Gebrselassie.

The World Championships turned out to be a runaway for the Kenyan team. Tergat's plan was to remain with the group until the last couple of kilometers, then slip away to capture his second world title. The first 10K went in 27:57, an unbelievable pace in cross country. In the 11th kilometer, when inevitable weariness was setting in, Tergat made his move. At the same moment, a tired Gebrselassie stumbled at a log obstacle; when he looked up, Tergat was gone. The last 1500 was run in 3:45 (equal to Tergat's track best)! Some observers mentioned that if Gebrselassie had not tripped then maybe the result would have been different. But cross country barriers, as in the steeplechase, are there to make the race more challenging. If you don't get over them properly, it is usually due to fatigue. Also, the stumble was a mere moment and the gap between them at the finish was 44 seconds (Gebrselassie finishing 5th).

Stramilano seemed a good site to exploit some of Tergat's wonderful form. Like many Kenyans, Paul is sponsored by Fila, the Italian clothing brand. So, Stramilano it was. Tergat knew he would fly on the roads, so he wasted no time on tactics. When the gun fired, he blasted away, covering the first 10km in 27:37 and 15km in under 42 minutes. The outstanding finishing time of 58:51 will not stand officially as the course was remeasured to be 49 meters short, equivalent perhaps to eight seconds.

The summer season was capped with Tergat's much-lauded silver medal at the Atlanta Olympics. Tergat had finished fourth, sufferering from cramps, behind Josephat Machuka, Paul Koech and William Kiptum in the Kenyan trials. His international experience and proven results, however, convinced the selectors to include him on the Olympic team.

The Olympic final saw Koech nobly handling the early work. Tergat took off with a 60-second lap with 2km to the finish. The last 2 kilometers were run in 5:05—a world class time for the distance. Gebrselassie, however, was able to outkick Tergat in the final 400m, though Paul held on very well to finish less than a second behind.

Many had predicted slow times in the distance events due to the sauna-like conditions in Atlanta. Thanks to the Kenyans, though, the results were swifter than expected. Koech and Tergat pulled the winner to an Olympic record. Tergat himself was rewarded with a personal best—albeit for just one month. In Brussels in August he became just the fifth man in history to break 27 minutes in the 10,000 meters.

Starting intensive training in November for the 1997 World Cross Country Championships, Tergat again reached superb form and raced to his third straight win. This time the margin over the runner-up (10,000m world record holder Salah Hissou of Morocco) was a bit closer (2 seconds), but it was a convincing victory for Tergat nonetheless. He took home $65,000—$40,000 for the world championship and then $25,000 for winning the 1997 IAAF Cross Challenge, his World Championship triumph moving him from sixth place to the Cross Challenge winner's circle.

| | |
|---|---|
| Date of birth | June 17, 1969. |
| Personal bests | 1500m—3:45.91, 2000m—5:01.5, 3000m—7:28.70, 5000m—12:54.72, 10,000m—26:54.41, 15K (road) — 42:13, half-marathon—59:56. |
| Honors won | 1996 Olympic 10,000m, 2nd |
| | World Cross Country champion 1995, 1996 and 1997. |
| | 1995 World Championships 10,000m, 3rd |
| | 3-time Stramilano Half-Marathon champion 1994, 1995, 1996 |
| | 1997 IAAF Cross Challenge champion. |
| Height/weight | 5-11¹/₂ (182cm), 137 lbs (62kg). |
| Home | House in Kabarnet. Apartment in N'gong Hills. |
| Coach | Self-coached. |
| Sponsor | Fila. |
| Family runners | Brother Douglas is a national-class runner. |
| Years running | "Many!" Started "serious" training in the winter of 1991-92. A former basketball player . |
| Occupation | Sergeant at Moi Air Force Base. Professional runner. His father takes care of some land investments. "In Kenya the economy is not as stable as the land." |
| Motivation | For 1996, it was to make the Olympic team and run well in the Games . |
| Family | Wife Monica, who is studying at college, and two children, Harriet and Rono. |
| Training sessions | Two per day. Usually the first run at 06.00 and the second at 10.00. "Like most Kenyans, I have trained three times a day, but I find two is enough." |
| Kilometers per week | 140. |
| Comments | "Go into competition with confidence from your training." Paul makes the point about specific training—look at what needs your event has and train accordingly. The balance between family and |

training is also important. "I live close to the Armed Forces camp, but not with the other runners. This suits me as if I need training partners, they are there, but it allows me to be with my family. I like to be able to relax with my family in front of the TV, playing with the kids. Determination, sacrifice, and discipline are three key words that crop up often when Tergat talks about his training background. "Without a lot of self-sacrifice I would never have made it. . . It takes discipline to train day in, day out. . . If you are not determined to do your best then it is better not to try at all." Tergat feels that a lot of Western athletes are too quick to erect mental barriers. "In Kenya there is the belief that if you train hard you will succeed. This we have proven."

## TRAINING SAMPLE

Quality is the watchword. The body should be fresh to be able to handle the speed sessions, Tergat believes. This is also the reason why he trains alone. "If I run with others then all sessions become full-speed burners; thus I prefer to run with others just for speed sessions."

Tergat does no long runs over 1 hr 30 min, believing that distance kills speed. "I hadn't trained too hard, but I knew I was in good shape," he said before the World Cross Country. Realizing weeks earlier at the nationals that he was in prime form, Tergat was careful just to maintain form and not tire himself with exhausting training. Basically he trains like the majority of Kenyan runners, mirroring the Armed Forces cross country training during the winter months.

## THE WEEK AROUND THE KENYAN NATIONALS

February 1996.

| Wed. | 06.00 | 60 min steady. |
| | 10.00 | 40 min steady. |
| Thurs. | 06.00 | 40 min steady. |
| | 10.00 | 30 min fartlek. |
| Fri. | 06.00 | Short jog. Rest day. |
| Sat. | | National Cross Country Championships, 1st. |
| Sun. | | Rest day. |
| Mon. | 10.00 | 60 min steady, hilly terrain. |
| Tues. | 10.00 | 60 min steady, hilly terrain. |

| Wed. | 06.00 | 60 min steady. |
| | 10.00 | 40 min fartlek, hard efforts. |
| Thurs. | 06.00 | 60 min steady. |
| | 10.00 | 30 min tempo. |
| Fri. | 06.00 | Short jog. Rest day. |
| Sat. | | IAAF Nairobi Cross Challenge, 1st. |

## Rose Cheruiyot

Rose Jelagat Cheruiyot is a vigorous and resolute athlete. Few drive themselves harder. Every morning during the cross country buildup period, a host of international stars can be found on the dirt roads of Iten for a "wake-up" run before the day's principal session. Some runners take it gently, most exert themselves moderately, one or two indulge in an arduous effort on occasion. But then there is Rose.

Charging along the roads dressed in her sponsor's track suit and red woolen hat, the young woman from Sabor makes each individual mile count. The concentration is chiseled into her perspiring brow. "I know the only way to success is through hard training. Before that we are all equal."

Rose Cheruiyot desperately wants to triumph on the track, to go where no other has before her in the 5000 meters. Her style of running has been very effective in cross country and road running.

After a disappointing 8th-place finish in the 1995 World Cross Country Championships, Cheruiyot lined up a week later at the Carlsbad 5000m road race on the advice of her manager, John Bicourt. He believed his athlete was ready to break through.

Rose did not impress until halfway through the race, when she put the "pedal to the metal," indeed catching some of the elite men's field as she strode toward the finish. Checking her watch every 500m, Rose had the world "record" in mind. "I was thinking 'yes—push hard, you can do it' and using the watch to see how close I was." Cheruiyot stopped the clock in 15:05, a new world best. Within ten minutes of crossing the finish line Rose had regained her breath and composure, leading the observer to wonder how fast she could have run if there had been any close challengers.

With the prospect of a handsome bonus from her sponsors, Rose entered the Cherry Blossom 10-mile road race the following week. Not only had she never competed over this distance, she had never run ten miles in training! The edge she had though was *belief*. "Before I even knew the time I had to beat I knew I could take the record." Determined words. The result was that Jill Hunter had to relinquish her world best that day to Rose.

Winning the World IAAF Cross Challenge in 1995/6 was another important milestone for Rose Cheruiyot. Since her serious career began as a junior in 1994 she has been a Kenyan stalwart, never failing to finish outside the top ten positions in the World Championships—cross country or track.

| | |
|---|---|
| Date of birth | July 21, 1976. |
| Birthplace | Sabor. Keiyo District. |
| Height/weight | 5-4½ (164cm), 108 lbs (49kg). |
| Personal bests | 1500m—4:16.41, 3000m—8:39.34, 5000m—14:46.41, 5K road—15:05 WB, 10km road—31:43, 10 miles road—51:40 WB. |
| Honors won | 1994 World Junior Cross Country Championships, 2nd |
| | 1996 World Cross Country Championships,2nd |
| | 1995 World Championships 5000m, 7th |
| | 1995 All-African Games: 5000m, 1st |
| | 1995 Kenyan national cross country champion |
| | World Cross Challenge: 1995, 2nd; 1996, 1st |
| | World road bests at 5000m and 10 miles (1995). |
| Home | Maisonette, St. Patrick's High School. Crystal Palace, London, during summer competition. |
| Family | Married to Ismael Kirui. |
| Sponsor | Nike. |
| Coach | Brother Colm O'Connell. |
| Years running | Began in 1993. "I lived a half kilometer from my school, so I am not one of those Kenyans who has been running to school throughout their childhood." |
| Reasons for beginning | "I saw the financial success of others and thought 'why not me?'" |
| Occupation | Professional athlete. |
| Training sessions | Two, sometimes three, per day. |
| Favorite sessions | Morning run, i.e., 40 min good steady pace. |
| Hardest session | Track intervals. "After 5x1000m I am dead!" |
| Motivation | Olympics and a world record in the 5000m on the track. |
| Best achievement | Junior world record in the 5000m, Cologne 1995. |
| Family runners | Rose has a younger sister who plans to begin training at the same age Rose was when she started. |
| Kilometers per week | Maybe around 90. Rose does not keep count. |
| Comments | Rose, like most elite Kenyans, believes in main- |

taining a training focus that should be 100% during the training period. "Try to put all of your energy into the training efforts and take them seriously." Cheruiyot never runs over one hour in training and likes to put in three interval sessions per week in the speed buildup part of her training. When preparing for her favorite event, cross country, Rose runs exclusively hill workouts and tempo runs, never taking to the track. "Become used to hardships and face them head on." Rose Cheruiyot has not reached the level she has by any path other than the hardest. "Before I won the Kenyan XC title in 1995 I had traveled through the night to get to Nairobi for the competition. I think I slept just two hours and was stiff from sharing my seat with two others in a jam-packed bus."

Beginning barefoot, then running in her everyday school shoes, Rose did not get her first pair of running shoes until the Embu training camp before the 1994 World Cross Country Championships. "I went for a schools competition in Australia when I first began running in 1993, but all I got was a t-shirt." With a lucrative contract secured from one of the primary sport shoe companies, Rose no longer has problems with lack of proper footwear. She has shown that where there is a will of iron there is a way of gold.

## TRAINING PROGRAM

Winter cross country training, January 1996. Location: Iten. Altitude: 2300m. Surface: red dirt roads.

Day 1   AM   11km hilly, good speed.   PM   6km top speed, hilly.
Day 2   AM   8km fast, strong effort.   PM   7km top speed.
Day 3   AM   8km fast "from the gun." PM   6km top speed.
Day 4   AM   Hill work, 10x200m steep incline, jog back down.
              20 min warm-up and warm-down at a good speed.
Day 5   AM   50 min fast, over hills.   PM   Travel to Eldoret.
Day 6   AM   8km steady.   MID   30 min steady.   PM   6km fast.
Day 7   AM   8km steady.   MID   30 min steady.   PM   7.7km fast.
Day 8   AM   8km steady.   MID   30 min steady.   PM   6km fast.
Day 9   AM   50 min fast, over hills.   PM   Rest, family business.
Day 10  AM   8km steady.   MID   30 min steady.   PM   6km FAST.

# SPRING TRAINING, PREPARING FOR TRACK SEASON

Location: Iten. Altitude: 2300m. Surface: red dirt roads and a rough "cow field" running track.

| | | | | |
|------|-----|------------------|-----|------------------|
| Day 1 | AM | 40 min good pace. | PM | 30 min steady. |
| Day 2 | AM | 8km steady. | PM | 10x200m, 200 jog rest. |
| Day 3 | AM | 8km steady. | PM | 4x800m (2:28, 2:29, 2:31 and 2:30) 2x600m (1:51 and 1:49) 1x400m (77), after 3 min rest. |
| Day 4 | AM | 8km steady. | PM | 30 min relatively easy. |
| Day 5 | AM | 8km fast. | PM | 30 min fast hilly route. |
| Day 6 | AM | 50 min fast. | PM | Rest. |
| Day 7 | AM | 8km steady. | PM | 5x400m and 5x200m, short jog rest. |

All the track sessions would usually include a 4km warm-up and cool-down run. The times for the intervals are not meaningful, due to the lung-searing altitude and the ankle-twisting running track. On Day 3, Rose was joined by Lydia Cheromei, herself in good form. Lydia was trailing by two seconds after the first interval, fifteen after the second and she quit on the third 800m interval!

# About The Author

Multifaceted is a term that can easily be applied to Toby Tanser. His *curriculum vitae* includes child actor, theater technician, published poet, pub musician, chef and professional road racer. He has lived in England, Holland, Iceland, and now Sweden. Born in Sheffield, England in 1968, Toby ran as a schoolboy but quit all sports until he returned to running as a 22-year-old smoker. While working in Iceland, he was undefeated in three years of cross country and road racing. Toby is now an athletic consultant to the Stockholm Athletic Association and still earns a living on the road racing circuit in Europe and America.